Next Generation Course Redesign

PETER LANG
New York • Washington, D.C./Baltimore • Bern
Frankfurt • Berlin • Brussels • Vienna • Oxford

PHILIP M. TURNER
RONALD S. CARRIVEAU

Next Generation Course Redesign

PETER LANG
New York • Washington, D.C./Baltimore • Bern
Frankfurt • Berlin • Brussels • Vienna • Oxford

Library of Congress Cataloging-in-Publication Data

Turner, Philip M.
Next generation course redesign / Philip M. Turner, Ronald S. Carriveau.
p. cm.
Includes bibliographical references and index.
1. Education, Higher—United States. 2. Curriculum change—United States.
3. General education—United States. 4. Academic achievement—United States.
I. Carriveau, Ronald S. II. Title.
LA227.4.T865   378.1'99—dc22   2009042668
ISBN 978-1-4331-0681-1

Bibliographic information published by **Die Deutsche Nationalbibliothek**.
Die Deutsche Nationalbibliothek lists this publication in the "Deutsche
Nationalbibliografie"; detailed bibliographic data is available
on the Internet at http://dnb.d-nb.de/.

Cover art inspired by the Next Generation Course Redesign logo,
© University of North Texas. Reprinted with permission.

The paper in this book meets the guidelines for permanence and durability
of the Committee on Production Guidelines for Book Longevity
of the Council of Library Resources.

© 2010 Philip M. Turner, Ronald S. Carriveau.
Peter Lang Publishing, Inc., New York
29 Broadway, 18th floor, New York, NY 10006
www.peterlang.com

All rights reserved.
Reprint or reproduction, even partially, in all forms such as microfilm,
xerography, microfiche, microcard, and offset strictly prohibited.

Printed in the United States of America

"To the faculty and staff whose creativity and perseverance pioneered the way for course redesign that will enhance learning for the next generation of students."

CONTENTS

INTRODUCTION		1
ONE	WHY COURSE REDESIGN?	3
	Higher Education and Change	3
	The Perfect Storm	5
	Success or lack thereof	5
	Demographics	6
	Financial	6
	Knowledge about students and how they learn	6
	Accountability	7
	Thriving in the Storm	8
	Conclusion	8
TWO	WHAT DO WE KNOW ABOUT COLLEGE STUDENTS AND HOW THEY LEARN?	9
	The Brain and Learning	9
	The role of neural networks	9
	Increasing the probability that learning occurs	11
	Role of the teacher	12
	Deep and Surface Learning	12
	Why is deep learning better than surface learning?	12
	Teaching for deep learning	14
	Student Engagement	14
	What is student engagement?	15
	How are students engaged?	15
	Cognitive Development	15
	Kegan's stages of cognitive development	16
	Encouraging cognitive development	16

	The Net Generation	17
	Characteristics of the Net Generation	17
	How do Millennials learn best?	18
	Conclusion	19
THREE	**THE NEXT GENERATION COURSE REDESIGN™ PROJECT**	**21**
	National Context of Course Redesign	21
	The Evolution of Course Redesign at UNT	22
	The Blended Learning Projects	22
	The QEP: Making Big Classes Better	24
	Next Generation Course Redesign™ emerges	25
	The Next Generation Course Redesign™ Process	25
	Goals of the NGen Process	25
	NGen Process logistics	26
	NGen Request for Proposals	27
	NGen Community of Practice	28
	Official NGen events and activities	28
	Retreats	29
	Monthly meetings	30
	Presentations to internal and external audiences	33
	Formal and informal training	34
	The NGen Course	35
	Goals of NGen courses	35
	Characteristics of an NGen course	36
	Carefully-crafted Student Learning Outcomes that include higher level learning	36
	An assessment plan with test items	37
	A research-based blend of instructional approaches	39
	Conclusion	40
FOUR	**OUTCOME BASED ASSESSMENT AND COURSE REDESIGN**	**41**
	Step 1: Developing the Outcome Statements	41
	Outcomes and Assessment Defined	41
	SLOs and measurability	42
	The goal-outcome hierarchy	42
	Possible sources for Goals, GO's and SLO's	43

	Step 2: Developing the Test Specifications Plan	44
	Step 3: Writing and Validating Test Items	45
	Item writing rules and guidelines for selected response and constructed response items	45
	Test score validity	45
	Validating selected response test items	46
	Validating constructed response test items	47
	Step 4: Evaluating Redesigned Courses and Programs	47
	Preference for course format	48
	Student attitude toward subject of the course	48
	Learning Environment Preferences (LEP) survey	48
	Final score distribution	49
	Outcome attainment values	49
	Surveys used to gather information for the evaluation of the N-Gen program	50
	Survey of Course Evaluation by Instructor Who Designed and Taught the Course	50
	Survey of Course Evaluation by Instructor Who Taught the Course But Did Not Design It	50
	Survey of Course Evaluation by Department Chairs and Deans of Redesigned Courses	50
	Adoption of Courseware Survey for Faculty Members	50
	Community of Practice Survey	51
	Conclusion	51
FIVE	ENABLING COURSE REDESIGN	53
	Barriers to Course Redesign	53
	Guidelines for a Successful Course Redesign Process	54
	Identify the problem and propose the solution (carefully)	54
	Select the right leader	55
	Plan for the long term	55
	Decide whether to target a single department or an entire institution	55
	Decide whether to redesign a single section or every section of the course	56
	Plan for the short term	57

Obtain support at all levels of the institution	58
Create an effective Community of Practice	59
Bring together faculty and support staff to ensure initial success	59
Provide the necessary support	60
Provide training	60
Provide structure	60
Provide incentives	61
Focus relentlessly on assessment	62
Get and keep the word out	63
Use a variety of channels and activities to disseminate course redesign project information	63
Address the scheduling and space challenges	64
Recognize and reward effective teaching	65
Changing the reward structure for tenured/tenure-track faculty	66
Developing a career track for instructors	66
Developing a separate administrative unit	66
Conclusion	67

SIX — NEXT GENERATION COURSE REDESIGN™ IN PRACTICE: FIVE CASES — 69

Case Study: Redesigning Principles of Biology I	70
Background of Redesign	70
Synopsis of Redesigned Course	70
Creating the Foundation: Student Learning Outcomes and Assessment	71
The Pedagogy	72
Lecture	73
Online	73
Recitation	74
Results	75
Concept inventory	75
Student success	76
Student Assessment of Learning Gains	76
Surveys	77
Sustainability and Replication	77
The N-Gen Process	78

CONTENTS

Case Study: Redesigning Communicating in Business	79
Background of redesign	79
Synopsis of redesigned course	79
Creating the foundation: Student learning outcomes and assessment	80
The Pedagogy	81
Pre-Tests and Post-Tests	82
Textbook readings	82
Lectures and in-class exercises	82
Team project	83
Online activities	84
Exams	84
Results	84
Evidence of student support for the innovation	84
Evidence that the innovation enhances teaching effectiveness	85
Evidence of peer recognition for the innovation	86
Sustainability and replication	86
The N-Gen process	87
Case Study: Redesigning Art History Survey II	89
Background of redesign	89
Synopsis of redesigned course	89
Creating the foundation: Student learning outcomes and assessment	91
Institutional	92
Departmental	93
Course	93
Module	94
The Pedagogy	96
Lectures	96
Online and other out of class activities	96
Small group work	97
PBL-inspired challenge	98
Results	98
Sustainability and replication	99
The N-Gen Process	100
Case Study: Redesigning World Literature	101
Background of redesign	101

Synopsis of redesigned course	101
Creating the foundation	102
The Pedagogy	104
Lecture	104
Online	105
Experiential small-group learning	105
Results	107
Summative Exams	107
Surveys	107
DFW Rates and Costs	110
Sustainability and replication	111
The N-Gen Process	111
Case Study: Redesigning U.S. History	112
Background of redesign	112
Synopsis of redesigned course	113
Creating the foundation: Student learning outcomes and assessment	114
The Pedagogy	115
Lecture	115
Online	118
Results	119
Sustainability and replication	120
REFERENCES	123
INDEX	127

INTRODUCTION

Higher education is facing a "perfect storm" of challenges. Enrollments and accountability are increasing while funding and the ability to raise tuition are decreasing. Students are arriving with learning behaviors increasingly incongruent with the mass lecture approach. Fortunately, developments in learning technologies and brain research provide the foundation to survive and even thrive in this storm.

The impetus and foundation of this book is the Next Generation Course Redesign™ Project at the University of North Texas in which for the past six years, faculty and staff have worked together to transform teaching and learning in large enrollment undergraduate courses. This book is part scholarly treatise, part chronology, and part how-to manual. It is meant to inform and inspire those who seek to enhance learning through making real changes in the design and delivery of the courses that are so crucial to providing a foundation of a successful college experience.

The book begins by providing a case for radically transforming teaching and learning in general education courses and then provides a rationale and a research-based blueprint for achieving this transformation. Next Generation Course Redesign™, a process that results in both an expanding Community of Practice and replicable validated courses, is described next. Chapter Four introduces the process through which Student Learning Outcomes for each course are developed and assessed as well as the various ways that the impact of the project itself is assessed. Significant institution-wide change is very difficult and the fifth chapter provides guidelines for increasing the probability of transformative course redesign. The final portion of the book was authored by the real heroes of course redesign –the faculty who describe their course redesign projects in Chapter 6.

Wherever you are in your course redesign journey, whether you are a college president seeking institution-wide change or a faculty member hoping to redesign one section of a class, we hope that this book will assist you. The Next Generation Course Redesign™ Project continues to evolve so please visit http://NGen.unt.edu to stay informed. Most importantly, please share your redesign experiences with us.

Transforming a significant portion of introductory undergraduate courses is a huge task, but the students in these classes represent our future. They need and deserve the best learning experience possible. The tools are available for the transformation. The will and the effort are what is refined.

· CHAPTER ONE ·

WHY COURSE REDESIGN?

This chapter discusses the degree to which higher education has changed in the past century, particularly as a result of the digital revolution. The convergence of disruptive forces is covered and the opportunity to address them in a way that will benefit this next generation is presented.

Higher Education and Change

Suppose a college professor or administrator from the early twentieth century could find a way to travel forward to today to study higher education one hundred years into the future. They would be amazed and, perhaps, disconcerted by our digital world. Developments in information technology and telecommunications have revolutionized the way that much of the population conducts business, elects a president, and is entertained. Developments in neuroscience and genetics have provided real insights into how humans learn.

Our time traveler finds their way to the college that they attended, noticing that it is now a "university", and enters with some trepidation, expecting to feel out of place. Indeed, observing students communicating through the use of small devices which they both speak into and move their fingers across in a blur of motion is disconcerting. Somewhat dazed, they enter a large lecture hall and are amazed by the white boards and pleasantly-colored projections of text and occasional images on the screen. Their initial conclusion is that higher education has changed dramatically in a century.

However, as our time traveler continues to observe the lecture, it becomes apparent that, although the means of delivering textual content has morphed from blackboard to computer projection, the basic faculty-centered pedagogy is the same. The instructor is still mainly dispensing content aurally, while students take notes. Learning is still largely a passive acquisition of content that is often retained only long enough to pass a test.

The core instructional activity in higher education has been amazingly resistant to change, as illustrated in Tapscott's (2008) recollection of the conversation between two college presidents about their faculty's teaching styles. One college president remarks that the faculty are teaching in a post-Gutenberg mode and the other replies, "Our model is pre-Gutenberg. We've got a bunch of professors reading from handwritten notes, writing on the blackboards, and the students are writing down what they say. This is a pre-Gutenberg model--the printing press is not even part of the learning paradigm" (p. 7).

So, is it true that the digital revolution has completely bypassed higher education? Of course it has not. Access to the Web is ubiquitous on most campus is Online courses, online programs, and even universities that are totally online are proliferating. But the International experience of most freshmen and sophomores remains unchanged. Occasionally, after considerable pressure from the administration, one section of a General Education course will be offered online, but carefully cordoned off from the "real classes". What is remarkable and tragically predictable is how each new technology is used to deliver lecture-dominated faculty-centered instruction. Videoconferencing allows faculty to lecture unfettered by distance. Podcasting removes the time as well as the distance limitations to lecturing.

An obsession with "coverage", prevalent in most general education classes, has also been particularly resistant to change. Some faculty are afraid to leave a topic out because their course is a prerequisite. Others are operating on an outdated learning model that posits that before one can think critically, one must possess all the facts. Most are laboring under the misconception that covering a concept, i.e., talking about it in a lecture, equates with the student acquiring and understanding the concept. Parini (2005) tells an interesting story of how Robert Frost teaching at Amherst College ninety years ago was considered somewhat eccentric for not following the text and for eschewing content as the goal of teaching. Frost's goal was to encourage critical thinking and the ability to present one's case in a convincing manner. More recently, Gardner (1993) observed,

> "The greatest enemy of understanding is coverage. I can't repeat that often enough. If you're determined to cover a lot of things, you are guaranteeing that most kids will not understand, because they haven't had time enough to go into things in depth, to figure out what the requisite understanding is, and be able to perform that understanding in different situations" (p. 24).

The Perfect Storm

So, why should higher education change a method of instruction that has withstood the test of time? As we close the first decade of the twenty-first century, there are forces impacting higher education that present an alternative to business as usual that is so compelling that real change is not only possible, it is probable. These forces include low success rates in general education classes, changing student demographics, skyrocketing costs, increased understanding of learning, and a call for colleges to provide evidence of the value that they add.

Success or lack thereof

One of higher education's dirty little secrets is the low percentage of students who succeed in general education courses. In many of these courses, over one-quarter of the students withdraw or receive grades of D or F. An alarming number of these courses have "non-success" rates of 40 or 50% percent. If a student does not succeed in a general education course, there are consequences for both the student and the institution, most of them bad. Many of these students are discouraged and drop out. In fact, students who performed well in introductory courses were twice as likely to complete the degree as their less successful counterparts (Adelman, 1999). Those who do not succeed and persist in the program must retake the course, taking a seat away from an entering student. Sometimes up to 50% of the seats in notorious "bottleneck" courses are taken up by repeaters.

It is often difficult to obtain the data on the percentage of students not succeeding at an institution. In the competition for revenue and gifts, bad publicity is shunned. The disclosure of the success rate often leads to denial and anger. General education instructors blame the high school preparation of their students and the blame cycles downward, often ending up with genes as the ultimate culprit.

Another explanation for the lack of success in introductory courses is the need to screen students for lack of effort or aptitude. There are a surprising number of faculty who are proud of the large percentage of students who do not succeed in their courses. However, as Seymour and Hewitt (1997) point out, a significant number of students who do not succeed have both aptitude and interest.

Demographics

Enrollment in higher education in the United States increased 23% between 1995 and 2005 (U.S. Department of Education, National Center for Education Statistics, 2008), and is projected to increase 13% during the next ten years. In addition, the student body will be much more diverse. The projected growth is 26% for black students and 39% for Hispanic (Hussar and Bailey, 2008). The growth is driven both by increasing college age populations and by the widespread belief that a college education is the ticket to a middle class lifestyle. In addition, the financial meltdown that began in 2007 has resulted in a wave of newly unemployed students straining an already overcrowded system at many colleges. For the foreseeable future, general education instructors will have a larger and more diverse enrollment in their classes.

Financial

Higher education is experiencing an expenditure growth curve that is not sustainable. Inflation-adjusted expenditures per student increased an astonishing 28 percent between 1990 and 2001 (U.S. Department of Education, National Center for Education Statistics, 2006). Little if any of this increase in cost per student can be attributed to the actual delivery of general education instruction. In fact, increasing use of non-tenure track instructors and ever-larger classes has made these classes one of the least cost-intensive ventures of a university. Whether it is a student services "space race," bloated administrative layering, declining state support, or another culprit, the fact is that there will be precious little funding to direct toward the problems with large enrollment classes.

Knowledge about students and how they learn

We probably all can recall our favorite lecture in college. Mine was on parasitic worms and to this day, I can recall the story of a person with trychanosis-infected eyelids. Lecturing is also deeply embedded in the psyche of the professoriate. As one of our colleagues commented, "It is the 'me' in teaching. "Lecture-based instruction is a highly efficient method of delivering content. The size of lecture-based classes can be increased without an impact on test results (Australian Universities Teaching Committees, 2003). Unfortunately, the effectiveness of lecture-based instruction is poor. There seems to be an upper limit of about

30 percent of content retention no matter how skilled the lecturer (Wieman, 2007). In addition, lecture seems to be particularly ineffective in enabling higher cognitive level learning (Australian Universities Teaching Committees).

The limitations of the lecture method are easily understood within the context of recent developments in cognitive science. Higher level learning is enhanced by an experience in which students are actively engaged with the content and with each other (Association for the Study of Higher Education, 2007). Unfortunately, as class sizes have grown, lecture rather than instructional methods that promote active and engaged learning, has been viewed as being the only feasible approach.

What is especially challenging is that outside of the classroom, today's college students are continuously engaged. They are used to operating in a digital environment that provides a multitude of choices rather than the "one-item" menu of content delivery found in general education classes. We may yearn for the days when students came to class "prepared to learn", i.e., listen and take notes, but instructors who ignore the fact that today's college students are natives from a digital world where communication is real time and multi-modal, face an increasing gap between their teaching and learning.

This gap and, the accompanying negative student reaction, is concisely illustrated in a video entitled, "A Vision of Students Today," (Wesch, 2007) created by Michael Wesch's and the two hundred students in his Introduction to Anthropology class. The four minute, forty second video shot in a typical sterile large lecture hall features bored students mutely revealing statements on how that environment is not amenable to their learning. Within a few months of its debut on YouTube, the video was viewed over 3,000,000 times. The more than 8,000 comments posted reveal the depth of feeling on both sides of the issue.

Accountability

Higher education will be held more accountable in the future. There are too many forces pushing in that direction for the trend to be reversed. Accrediting agencies have been a major force and the Federal Government has entered the fray seemingly determined to force quicker action in this area. Ultimately, though, it will be those who pay tuition who will be the most demanding. In 2008, the cost of higher education rose at a higher rate (5.8%) than any other product or service, while the CPI fell at an annual rate of 13% (Coy, 2009). There are already moves by state legislatures to move to a success-based funding model and away from enrollment based.

Thriving in the Storm

We know how important general education courses are. Two thirds of the gains that students make in knowledge and cognitive skill development occur in the first two years of college (Pascarella and Terenzini, 2005). We are facing a "perfect storm" of factors that make transforming these classes both imperative and challenging. An unacceptably large percentage of students are not succeeding in these classes and either dropping out of college or clogging up the system by repeating the course.

We are faced with an entrenched methodology, the lecture, that is not appropriate for teaching the critical thinking skills necessary to thrive in the 21st Century nor is it congruent with the digital natives entering higher education today. Finally, we will be required to teach more students with less resources and to be held accountable for the results.

Higher education is indeed facing myriad challenges that, collectively, may seem insurmountable. The good news is that while there is a cascade of problems facing us, there is also a "grand conjunction" of tools and opportunities. First, we know that if we provide an active learning experience that allows students to engage with the content, each other, and instructors, they can and will think critically and develop cognitively. Second, the digital revolution has provided the tools to deliver the foundational content effectively so that students, even in large classes, can work in small groups to master higher level learning. Third, there seems to be an emerging national awareness that a true transformation and not a "tinkering around the edges" of how general education courses are taught is needed now.

Conclusion

Higher education has an extraordinary opportunity, one not available even a decade ago, to seriously engage in the transformation of the undergraduate experience and, ultimately, to change how learning occurs throughout the institution. This book will provide a model on how to thrive in the storms and challenges facing us.

· CHAPTER TWO ·

WHAT DO WE KNOW ABOUT COLLEGE STUDENTS AND HOW THEY LEARN?

This chapter addresses the knowledge base necessary to redesign general education courses to meet the challenges facing higher education today. Major developments in how learning occurs and is promoted, including brain research, deep learning, and the impact of engagement are covered. Promoting cognitive development and the impact of the digital revolution on today's student will also be considered.

The Brain and Learning

We start learning before birth and continue until we die but until recently, the actual mechanics of learning were a mystery. Teaching activities and learner behaviors could be observed but what went on inside the student's head could only be inferred. Breakthroughs in medical technology, including brain imaging, have opened a window on the actual mechanics of learning and we now know that *all learning is biology*, and unless there is a biological change in the brain, learning has not occurred.

The role of neural networks

Everything that we know is represented by one or more neural networks and the more complicated the learning, the more complicated the networks. Wolfe (2001) describes three levels of neural networks that enable and

SCHEMA FOR THE RULE
The net force of an object is determined by the product of its mass times its acceleration

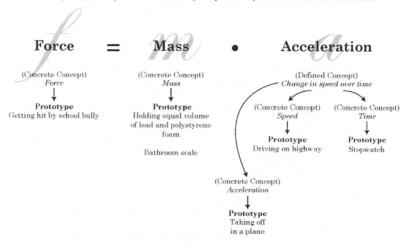

Figure 1 Schema Representing Neural Network of a Rule

correspond to different types of learning. The lowest level consists of the concrete concepts, the next level of neural network holds symbolic representations such as pictures and diagrams, and the highest and most complex level embodies abstractions.

Turner and Riedling (2003), use schemas to represent the neural networks formed when learning at each of Gagné's (1985) six levels of learning. Figure 1 depicts the schema for the rule: "The force of an object is determined by the product of its mass times its acceleration." This rule is a combination of two concrete concepts (force and mass) and a defined concept (acceleration).

Learning this rule at this particular level would require development/linking of neural networks in the brain represented in the schema. Zull, in his book, *The Art of Changing the Brain* (Zull, 2002), makes a very important point. Every network can ultimately be traced back to an experiential referent, because every idea we possess, no matter how abstract, is based on a concrete experience. Learning occurs when neural networks are created and/or linked and this happens at the individual level. Learners construct what they know by making connections and it is the teacher's role to create the circumstances that increase the probability that these connections are made.

Increasing the probability that learning occurs

Humans are designed to receive stimuli rapidly, but it takes considerable time and effort integrating the stimuli to make meaning. This integration involves a part of the brain that is limited in size but extremely fast at processing information. Ultimately, through processing external stimuli and retrieving stimuli from existing neural networks (also known as "thinking"), new networks and connections are created. A critical component of this sense making is a connection to something that is already known and ultimately to an experience that engages emotion.

We form many new neural networks every day but most of them quickly become dormant and difficult to retrieve. Which networks are maintained? Zull, answers this question succinctly, "Networks that fired together got wired together."(p. 118). Learning is maintained if the neural networks are activated repeatedly, including all of the relevant networks. In the example of learning the rule for force, simply activating the linkage to the rule itself, i.e., stating the rule verbally or in writing, is not sufficient for learning at the higher cognitive level. The networks for each concrete concept as well as for the defined concept acceleration would need to be activated so that the connections would be reinforced and, ideally, linked to other networks.

Therefore, putting what we learn to practice is critical. Zull calls for a minimum of requiring learners to write about what they are learning, using full sentences and paragraphs. Also important is defending conclusions, asking questions, and seeking more information. Erlauer (2003) recommends collaborative learning to strengthen neural network connections for the following reasons:

- Collaborative learning provides the brain with the means to explore new information in a problem-solving situation.
- The brain is social and learning with others is beneficial.
- Working with others tends to elicit emotions which can strengthen neural networks.
- Collaborative teamwork toward a goal stimulates the brain connections.
- Supportive collaborative work tends to be non threatening which facilitates the use of frontal cortex higher-level thinking.

Zull also promotes experiential learning activities involving peers because peers are most likely to have similar neural networks.

Role of the teacher

At the end of his book, Zull describes the emotions, so critical to enhancing changes in the brain, which a student goes through in the learning process. These begin with Inertia/Disinterest/Frustration, proceed to Uncertainty/Anxiety, and move on to Interest/Progress/Hope, and finally to Confidence/Success/Motivation. The role of the teacher is most important in the first three stages. Ultimately, as Zull points out, the goal is to bring the student to the point where they believe that they learned by themselves. This is accomplished by challenging the student, providing the optimum combination of examples and support, and finally stepping aside because the only true and lasting learning occurs when students make their own meaning.

Deep and Surface Learning

An important and logical way of looking at learning has been developed around the concepts of deep and surface learning. In addition to the intuitive appeal of this characterization, there is an obvious connection to the most common taxonomies of learning and to emerging brain research.

Why is deep learning better than surface learning?

Deep learning is at its essence making meaning through thinking. Ramsden (2003) provides a useful list of characteristics of both deep and surface approaches to learning (p. 47). A surface approach:

- Focuses on signs
- Focuses on unrelated parts
- Memorizes for assessment
- Fails to distinguish examples from principles
- Treats the task as an internal imposition

While a deep approach:

- Focuses on what is signified and the applicable concepts
- Relates previous knowledge
- Relates theoretical ideas
- Organizes structure into coherent wholes

Biggs and Tang (2007) describe teacher behaviors that encourage surface or deep learning. These can be paraphrased as either surface or deep learning teacher activities. Surface learning teacher activities:

- Teaching piecemeal and not bringing out the intrinsic structure of the subject
- Assessing for independent facts
- Lacking enthusiasm for the topic
- Emphasizing coverage versus depth
- Creating an anxious or overly stressful environment

Deep learning teacher activities:

- Explicitly providing the structure of the topic
- Eliciting active responses from the students
- Connecting what the students already know to what is to be learned
- Helping students identify and confront misunderstandings
- Assessing to emphasize structure rather than individual facts
- Encouraging an environment in which learning from mistakes is the norm
- Teach and assess in ways that support the student learning outcomes

Biggs and Collis (1982) describe five categories of complexity of learner responses. The first three, Prestructural (the use of irrelevant information), Unistructural (Focusing on one relevant aspect only), and Multistructural (focusing on several relevant but uncoordinated features) are typical results from surface learning. The last two categories, Relational (integrating several parts into a coherent whole with details linked to conclusions and sense making) and Extended Abstract (Generalizing the structure beyond the information given and using higher-order principles to introduce new and broader issues) are the result of deep learning.

The superiority of deep learning is obvious. Just over a decade ago, the Boyer Commission on Educating Undergraduates in the Research University (1998) took higher education to task for the neglect of undergraduate education and the reliance on teaching and testing methods that are clearly more aligned with surface rather than deep learning. From a brain-based learning perspective, striving for deep learning is important because it facilitates creating and sustaining more complex and useful neural networks. This complexity is the foundation for higher level learning and critical thinking.

Teaching for deep learning

Methods and activities that encourage an intention to understand rather than regurgitating facts facilitate deep learning. Unfortunately, since the practice is so widespread, lecture seldom leads to deep learning. To increase the probability that deep learning will occur, an instructor should encourage and enable active and independent learning. This is not easy, especially in ever-larger general education classes, but deep learning is about connecting internal and external phenomena in a way that is deeply personal and idiosyncratic.

Smith and Colby (2007) call for instructors to engage in a dialog about how deep learning might be represented in their discipline. It is clear that both the student learning outcomes and the assessment portions of a course are as critical as the methods to ensure that deep learning occurs.

Student Engagement

We all want our students to achieve academically and persist to complete their chosen program. Admission standards including high school grades and entrance exam scores are used to help ensure that students who are admitted will succeed. Many of these standards are coming under scrutiny because of bias and this scrutiny will increase as the college population becomes larger and more diverse.

Recently, the focus has shifted from the characteristics of entering students to what happens to students once they are in college. What impact does engaging students in meaningful academic activities have on their success and persistence? Reason, Terenzini, and Domingo (2006) concluded, based on a study of 6,700 students and 5,000 faculty members, that experiences in college is much more highly related to academic competence than the characteristics of entering students. These findings were echoed by Kuh, et al. (2008) who concluded that engaging students in purposeful educational activities had a positive and statistically significant impact on both first year grades and persistence in college after pre-college variables such as entrance exam scores were accounted for.

What is student engagement?

Building on what we know about brain-based as well as deep versus surface learning, it is logical that a cognitively-engaged student is one who is making meaning by expanding upon the knowledge structures provided to them. There is also a socially-engaged student who has developed relationships with faculty and peers. The best known institutional measure of student engagement is the National Survey of Student Engagement (NSSE http://nsse.iub.edu/index.cfm) and this instrument includes measures of both types of engagement.

How are students engaged?

Chickering and Gamson (1987) describe seven educational activities that they put forth as "good practice" in undergraduate education and these principles form the foundation for student engagement. Students in institutions in which these activities take place are more likely to be engaged in purposeful and beneficial learning activities. The activities are:

- student-faculty contact
- cooperation among students
- active learning
- prompt feedback
- time on task
- high expectations
- respect for diverse talents and ways of learning

Student engagement, and specifically an emphasis on higher-order thinking skills, active learning, and high expectations in general education courses, is important in achieving academic competence and in persistence in college. It is clear that if colleges can engage students in these purposeful educational activities, the educational "playing field" can be leveled.

Cognitive Development

For a long time, guided by the stages put forth by Piaget, we believed that students entering our doors had already reached the highest level of cognitive development. We have now moved to a post-Piaget view of meaning making, one that extends cognitive growth well into adulthood. According to this view, the majority of entering students are not at a cognitive level where we can fulfill the lofty goals found in our institutional mission and goal statements.

Kegan's stages of cognitive development

Robert Kegan (1994) extended Piaget's work and added stages of development that can occur well into adulthood. It is the transition from the third to the fourth stage and the critical role that general education must play that is of particular importance in this book.

Most entering college freshman have reached Kegan's third level or "interpersonal" stage. They can generalize from concrete examples to the abstract. They understand that there are multiple perspectives or opinions on a topic. Students at the third order of development lack an awareness of the "fragility" of authority and tend to look to others in an absolute sense as they make meaning. As an example, third-level students studying Manifest Destiny in an introductory U.S. History class can understand and appreciate that there were a variety of governmental and personal views regarding the divine right of the United States to expand. However, students at the third level seek authority that will tell them which perspective "is right."

At the fourth order of consciousness (Kegan's self authoring stage), the student makes the transition to ambiguity as a constant. They reflect on multiple perspectives as an important part of making their own meaning. The authority for constructing meaning has moved from external to internal along with an awareness of this shift. Students in our U.S. History class who are operating at the fourth level will understand that often historical "truth" is elusive. They understand that internalizing the process of history by experiencing a variety of viewpoints is what is critical.

Simply aging is not a guarantee that someone will make the transition from the third to the fourth level. In fact, neither an undergraduate or even a graduate degree assures or even makes this transition probable. Manwaring (2006), points out that Kegan estimates that only about one-third to one-half of the general adult population fully constructs meaning at the fourth order and only about one half of all graduate students do so.

Encouraging cognitive development

A natural and crucial role of the college experience is to provide a bridge between the third and fourth levels of cognitive development. Kegan (1994) challenges higher education to create a way to bring students across the "chasm" rather than assuming that they will make the transition simply by attending college. Unfortunately, the most common method of instruction, the lecture, reinforces the third level by emphasizing authority and dissemination of facts. Hodge, Lepore, Pasquesi, and Hirsh (2008) describe and promote a Student as Scholar model in which the learner is guided across the bridge to a reliance on self as source of authority. This is done through creating experiences that allow the students to author their own knowledge through sense making.

Hodge et al. recommend that foundational courses be a balance of the discipline and inquiry. These courses should be "infused" with a culture of inquiry that prepares students for advanced courses which will enable the transition to the fourth level of development. They point out that technology is an enabler that has made available an incredible variety of primary sources and authentic experiences. First and second year courses can serve as a bridge to the Student as Scholar model by providing research scaffolding, such as access to a limited number of primary source documents rather than or, in addition, to the textbook.

The Net Generation

Are students entering higher education today different in fundamental ways that might engender a substantial disjoint with the prevalent pedagogies? Writers such as Marshal McLuhan (McLuhan and Fiore, 1967) have told us that the medium through which we discourse can have a profound impact on us. Can it be that the digital revolution has so fundamentally altered the perception and communication of reality that humans who have grown up in a digital world have significantly different ways of communicating than those who did not? Tapscott (2009) makes the case that, "There are many reasons to believe that what we are seeing is the first case of a generation that is growing up with brains that are wired differently." (p. 29)

Characteristics of the Net Generation

Tapscott observes about Net Geners that "They seem to behave, and even to be different." (p. 10) They are also the largest generation in U.S. history surpassing even the baby boomers. They have grown up immersed in the

Web and citizenship in a digital world is taken for granted. Media are seen as participatory in ways never imagined just a few years ago. They have received a degree of parental attention previously unheard of. In addition, Tapscott (p. 34–35) purports that members of this generation:

- Scrutinize everything
- Want to be engaged and motivated
- Are more tolerant of diversity
- Are intolerant of slow response anywhere in their lives
- Are naturally social rather than individual
- Are virtual and social tinkerers
- Are smarter

How do Millennials learn best?

Interestingly, the very nature of life in a digital world with its individually incomplete and collectively inconsistent sources of information would seem to push a learner to Kegan's fourth level of cognitive development. In a world of Wiki's, everyone and no one is an authority.

While millennials have been immersed in digital technologies and are constantly communicating, often with several parties simultaneously, they like structure and a certain amount of face-to-face learning. However, face-to-face does not include lecture but rather working in teams on experiential hands-on tasks that are seen to be authentic. Millennials present a significant challenge to general education faculty, especially in large enrollment classes. These students need to master the art of reflection that the brain needs to make sense out of stimuli arriving from many sources. They need to develop an awareness of when "unplugging" is required and a willingness to do so (Pardue and Morgan, 2008).

At the close of the chapter on the Net Geners as learners, Tapscott (p. 148) provides tips for educators. These include:

- Use technology wisely to create a student-focused collaborative environment.
- Reduce lecturing and increase involvement of students in designing their learning
- Empower students to collaborate
- Focus on learning not on testing

- Use technology to get to know students
- Build customization, transparency, integrity, collaboration, fun, speed, and innovation into project-based learning
- Reinvent yourself

Conclusion

College faculty have an opportunity to know so much more than they could even a decade ago about how their students learn. If they truly want their students to "see the whole rather than the parts," to "make connections," and to leave the class with an increased interest in and, maybe even a little passion for, the subject, most will have to radically change their pedagogy. They will have to find ways to have students engage with the content, with each other, and with them. Active learning and collaborative learning will need to make up a significant amount of the class time. A wide range of digital tools must be considered and integrated into the class. Structure and freedom to learn must be carefully balanced to provide controlled creative chaos necessary for making meaning. Of course, all of this must be done within cost and logistical constraints.

· CHAPTER THREE ·

THE NEXT GENERATION COURSE REDESIGN™ PROJECT

This chapter provides the context and history of the Next Generation Course Redesign™ Project at the University of North Texas. The various steps are described through which courses are transformed and faculty become course redesign leaders. Finally, this chapter provides information on the blend of three instructional approaches that lead to engagement and deep learning in NGen courses.

National Context of Course Redesign

There have been a number of efforts to bring engagement and active learning into the curriculum. Hodge, Lepore, Pasquesi, and Hirsh (2008) call for moving away from an Instructional Paradigm, through the Learning Paradigm, to a Discovery Paradigm that features the student as scholar. Richard Freeland in his 2009 article subtitled, "The Necessary Revolution in Undergraduate Education," calls for making experiential and active learning a central part of the undergraduate experience.

What is particularly discouraging is that neither of these articles calls for transforming what takes place *inside* the classroom. Involving students in research, civic engagement and study abroad activities are mentioned as possible activities. Off campus employment is also put forward but considered perhaps too radical! It is encouraging that the need for a "revolution" is acknowledged but how can a revolution occur without addressing the college classroom, the main source of intellectual content?

Fortunately, there are projects that involve a real transformation of the instructional experience. This is particularly true in the sciences. Carl Wieman (2007) brought to course redesign the same dedication to evidence-based decisions that he brought to his Nobel Prize winning research in Physics. He points out that students learn physics not by listening to someone talk about it but by doing physics. While the most effective way to teach introductory physics would be to put students to work in small groups in his laboratory, he recognizes that logistical and fiscal constraints prevent this. Dr. Wieman and his colleagues have developed an experiential learning approach to introductory physics that combines online modules with small group classroom activities. Rimer (2009) describes an application of this approach at MIT that replaces large lectures with smaller class and much more interactive learning. This blending of instructional approaches was validated recently in the results of a meta-analysis which found that instruction that combined face-to-face and online approaches was superior to a single approach (Means, Toyama, Murphy, Bakia, and Jones, 2009).

The National Center for Academic Transformation (NCAT http://www.center.rpi.edu/) has been the leader in an effort to change the way in which introductory courses are taught. NCAT has managed a series of projects in which faculty used one of five models for redesigning the instructional approach and assessing the results of the redesign. In the past few years, NCAT has increased the number of institutions with which it is working and has begun working with university and college systems and state educational agencies.

This book is focused on a redesign project in which the University of North Texas has been engaged for several years. The Next Generation Course Redesign™ Project uses a multi-year process to transform and assess every aspect of a course from the student learning outcomes to the classroom activities.

The Evolution of Course Redesign at UNT

The Blended Learning Projects

The 2009–2010 Academic Year marked the sixth year of course redesign at the University of North Texas. While the Next Generation Course Redesign™ Project is a highly-structured very ambitious campus-wide project, course redesign at UNT began with far less ambition and structure. The initial idea for course redesign emerged as the Web blossomed in the 1990's. We began to realize that the learner-centered constructivist approach to instruction promoted in the literature for decades could actually be a possibility, even in the face of increasing enrollment and dwindling resources. By the spring of 2004, we had put together enough funding to offer grants to allow faculty from five undergraduate courses to spend the 2004–2005 Academic Year thinking about how to best blend face-to-face and online learning.

We had no agenda beyond improving success rates and there was very little structure to the process which we called, "The Blended Learning Project". The instructors responsible for each course received a small grant to buy out of teaching, hire graduate or undergraduate students to help them research the instructional content of their course, or to do anything else they believed would assist them to redesign their course. We decided that we would meet once a month over lunch to discuss redesign ideas and progress. The first five courses were:

- Introduction to Communication
- U.S. History I
- Principles of Language Study
- Music Appreciation
- Principles of Nutrition

We still call that first year our "Woodstock". It was a semi-accidental coming together of people with passion about introductory college classes and carried out with a minimum of organization but with a commitment to learning. The lunch meetings often extended well beyond the allotted time and were filled with sometimes simultaneous discussions and exchanging of ideas. We were fortunate to have several very creative and organized faculty who emerged as leaders and role models. We also knew that if we wanted to be able to continue and expand this project, we needed to publicize it and bring it to the attention of the administration.

During this first year, there was a growing awareness on campus of many of the negative forces described in Chapter One. Enrollment was surging along with class size. There were frank and painful discussions at the highest levels regarding the large percentage of students in general education courses who were not succeeding. Inflation adjusted State financial support was declining and increasingly tied to performance criteria that included "student throughput" measures such as time to graduation.

Impressed by demonstrations of the redesigns of the original five courses, the provost offered to support the redesign of four courses in a second year of the Blended Learning Project and an RFP was issued to the faculty in the spring of 2005. The RFP specifically targeted undergraduate courses with sections that had enrollments of 100 or more. In the fall of 2005, the redesign process used the preceding year was repeated and involved instructors from four large enrollment classes including:

- Principles of Biology
- The Science and Technology of Musical Sound
- Occupational Health: Lessons from Music
- Human Development

While the redesign of this second cohort of courses was underway, the faculty who had redesigned their class during Blended Learning I taught the redesign for the first time. Two of the redesigns, U.S. History I and Music Appreciation, were especially innovative and successful and these provided a model for the next cohort of faculty.

The QEP: Making Big Classes Better

In the summer of 2005, the University of North Texas was at the point in the SACS Reaffirmation Process in which a Quality Enhancement Plan (QEP) had to be selected. After considerable discussion, a university-wide committee selected the goal of enhancing student learning outcomes in large enrollment undergraduate classes as the QEP Topic. Eighteen months of experience in the Blended Learning Project informed by the stringent assessment requirements of SACS resulted in a proposal submitted to and approved by SACS with very positive comments by the visiting team. The proposed five-year project involved the redesign, implementation, and assessment of at least twenty-four large enrollment general education classes to improve student learning outcomes. In the spring of 2006, an RFP solicited proposals for the first five courses to be redesigned as part of the QEP and a QEP Advisory Committee selected the following courses to be redesigned during the first year of the QEP:

- Art History Survey II
- Computer Applications
- General Chemistry for Science Majors
- World Literature I
- Communicating in Business

Next Generation Course Redesign™ emerges

Systematic course redesign at UNT, which began as the Blended Learning Project and developed into our QEP, was aided by over $2,000,000 in external grants during the first three years. This support enabled our approach to course redesign to evolve into something unique and very exciting. We realized that we had created the next generation of course redesign, a process that would result in a suite of high-quality tested courses and learning objects to teach the next generation of college students.

The Next Generation Course Redesign™ Process

Five years of course redesign work has produced a model for the process of bringing together the people and resources necessary to undertake and sustain transformational course redesign . This model recognizes that real course redesign is not easy; it requires a significant long-term commitment by the instructor and involves a transformation of almost every aspect of the traditional general education course. More importantly, it requires a break from the comfort of teaching as one was taught and involves considerable risk taking. This model also makes the course redesign process a highly public undertaking in which each participant is strongly encouraged to document and reflect upon their activities.

Goals of the NGen Process

Although support from all levels of the academic administration is very important, the NGen process is largely a "bottom up" approach. Rather than mandating that all sections of a course be redesigned and delivered in the same way, we begin with one or two sections of a course and work with a few instructors to redesign, teach, assess, improve, and make available a well-designed vibrant version of the course including digital learning objects, experiential learning activities, and lecture guides. The redesigned courses can be used in either a "turn-key" mode or to be modified and adapted by another instructor.

The goals of the NGen Process include (See Figure 1):

- Adopting "never-ending course redesign" in which the assessment, reflection, redesign process is sustained through multiple iterations by the original instructor
- Replicating the redesign through the adoption and adaption of the redesigned course by instructors of other sections of the course

UNT NGEN PROJECT GOALS

Figure 1 Goals of the NGen Process

- Creating and sustaining a thriving Community of Practice (CoP) around course redesign that includes faculty committed to and trained for leadership in course redesign
- Impacting teaching and learning at all levels throughout the institution and beyond

NGen Process logistics

The main focus of the NGen process involves a carefully choreographed series of events that begins with recruiting and selecting the courses and redesign faculty and ends with a proven high-quality course ready for adoption and adaption by others teaching the same course and with an experienced and committed faculty expert. In actuality, the process can and does extend beyond the two "official" years. As an example, Dr. Lee Hugh's Principles of Biology (originally redesigned in Blended Learning I) has been continuously undergoing a teaching/evaluation/redesign cycle for five years. The following are the most important events in the crucial first two years of the NGen process. (See http://NGen.unt.edu/go/BookMaterials for a two-year NGen calendar of events.)

NGen Request for Proposals

The NGen cycle begins with the issuing of an RFP in April to solicit proposals for participation in the upcoming year's NGen process (See http://NGen.unt.edu/go/BookMaterials for a sample RFP.) The requirements for a successful proposal include:

- Identification of an introductory undergraduate course with a section that has a large enrollment ("Large" is interpreted as being over 100 students. There can be a total of 100 students in multiple sections if the plan is to combine sections in the redesigned course)
- Identification of need for course redesign (problems with existing course)
- Evidence of willingness to participate in the Community of Practice including attendance at monthly working lunches or breakfasts, retreats, and faculty forums
- Evidence of understanding of the Next Generation Course Redesign Process and willingness to participate throughout the process
- Evidence of willingness to create and participate in a rigorous assessment of the redesigned course
- Commitment by the department chair and dean to redesign of the course

Applicants are strongly encouraged to attend the April NGen Faculty Forum featuring course redesign faculty who have successfully completed the redesign process.

The proposals are reviewed and ranked by an advisory board with representatives from each academic unit, the faculty senate the student government association, the graduate student association, and the library. The advisory board has three ex-officio members including the NGen Director (also the Director of UNT's QEP), an associate director, and a learning enhancement specialist). The Provost makes the final selection of the NGen courses.

The faculty whose proposals are selected are designated "Faculty Fellows" and awarded a grant of $12,000 for the upcoming fiscal year for each course. If instructors proposed as a team around a course, they divide the funding. The funds can be used to buy a course release, to hire student research or development support, or other uses agreed upon between the Faculty Fellows and the NGen staff. Funding for the Faculty Fellows is released in thirds and contingent upon satisfactory progress in the NGen redesign process. There have been cases, fortunately only a few, in which funding was terminated and the faculty "uninvited" because they found that they could not fulfill their responsibilities as a Faculty Fellow.

At the same time, Faculty Fellows from the previous year who have successfully completed the first year, and whose redesign meets the NGen standards are invited to become Senior Faculty Fellows and continue in the second year with offering, assessing, and continued redesigning of their course. This leadership status carries with it an award of $2,000 for the first year and $1,000/year award for each subsequent year of participation. Each Senior Faculty Fellow is presented with a contract letter that delineates the activities expected (See http://NGen.unt.edu/go/BookMaterials for sample contract letter.) To date every person invited to become or remain a Senior Faculty Fellow has accepted. The Senior Faculty Fellows serve as models and ambassadors for the NGen Project.

NGen Community of Practice

Each year, Faculty Fellows become the newest members of the NGen Community of Practice, an informal, dynamic group dedicated to course redesign at UNT. The NGen CoP consists of the Faculty Fellows, Senior Faculty Fellows, NGen staff, and support personnel including the measurement and assessment specialist, faculty development specialist, instructional consultants, and librarians. The vitality and organizational context for the NGen CoP is measure through the use of a survey adapted, with permission, from Cross, R., T. Laseter, A. Parker, and B. Velasquez. (2004). Assessing and improving communities of practice with organizational network analysis. Retrieved December 10, 2009 from https://webapp.com.virginia.edu/NetworkRountable/Portals/0/Formalizing Communities of Practice Rountable Final.pdf

Official NGen events and activities

NGen course redesign is very challenging and takes considerable commitment and perseverance by each faculty fellow. This is particularly true because many of the fellows are the first in their department to redesign a course and even if a team of instructors are redesigning a course, they represent a small minority of from their department. Therefore, one of the goals of the NGen process is to engender an identity and pride in the fellows and throughout the CoP. NGen shirts(See Figure 2) and pens help to do this as well as photos on the official web site and continuing stories. Faculty Fellows are encouraged to contact each other and any of the support staff at any time. Scheduled events and activities also promote contact among the NGen CoP.

Figure 2 NGen Faculty Fellow

Retreats

The NGen year begins with an all-day retreat in August and the new Faculty Fellows are provided with readings on course redesign and assessment before the retreat. Topics for the retreat typically include:

- Review of the two-year NGen calendar
- Faculty Fellow responsibilities
- Content Mapping
- Student Learning Outcomes
- Assessment training schedule
- Intellectual property agreements
- Demonstrations by Senior Faculty Fellows of previously redesigned courses

The highlight of the retreat is a working lunch to which the President, Provost, Provost staff, deans and department chairs that represent that year's courses to be redesigned are invited. Each Faculty Fellow is introduced and talks about the course they plan to redesign. The lunch concludes with a demonstration of an NGen course by a Senior Faculty Fellow.

Faculty Fellows also attend a retreat in January of the first redesign year at which they present the SLO's and assessment plans for the redesigned course. At this retreat, production staff demonstrate a range of learning object options and a Senior Faculty Fellow demonstrates and discusses their NGen course (See Figure 3).

During the second year, Senior Faculty Fellows attend an "End of Course" Retreat in January in which they share the experiences, assessment results, and lessons learned from piloting the redesigned course in the fall. A final retreat in the summer of the second year provides the Senior Faculty Fellows with the opportunity to look back on two iterations of offering the redesigned course and forward to ways in which the course will continue to be improved and made available to others in their department.

Monthly meetings

The most important continuing event during the initial year in the NGen redesign process is the monthly meeting of Faculty Fellows. These meetings involve logistics including deadlines for submission of course materials and budget requirements. They also provide opportunities for training in crucial aspects of course redesign and for presentations of NGen courses by Senior Faculty Fellows. Most importantly, these sessions provide time for the Faculty Fellows to bring each other up to date on their course redesign and to share

Figure 3 NGen Senior Faculty Fellow

ideas, fears, and hopes about the courses they are redesigning. We have found that each successful Faculty Fellow has an "ah ha" moment during a second semester monthly meeting and that this moment of insight is often the result of exchanges with other fellows. As an example, the American Government redesign team created an experiential learning activity to support the student learning outcomes, "Describe ideologies and theories necessary for understanding American political thought and democratic theory." and "List and describe the key components of a democratic government. In other words, what makes a democracy?" They brought the draft in Figure 4 to the monthly meeting.

In the discussion that ensued, one of the Faculty Fellows suggested that this "active writing exercise" could be made more active, even in this class of one hundred and eighty students, and this led to a brainstorming session that resulted in the outline of a simulation game combining online and in-class elements (See Figure 5).

The Exercise: Promoting Democracy (First Draft)

You are an advisor to the newly elected President of the United States. One of his/her campaign goals is to promote the development of democratic governments around the world in a peaceful way. Some governments are more democratic than others, while some are not democratic at all. The President wants you to develop a list of the countries that are in the most need of democratic development. Utilizing a list of ten countries, prepare a memo to the president and develop a list of countries most in need of his attention. In your analysis be prepared to:

- Define the current form of government.
- Utilizing Huntington's definitions of a democracy, determine if each country matches the definition? Justify your answer and explain to the President why he/she should or should not worry about that country.
- If a country does not fit the definition of democracy, make suggestions to assist the county to become more democratic.
- Prioritize and justify an action list for the President.

Figure 4 First Draft` of Experiential Learning Activity

The Exercise: Promoting Democracy (Revised)

This is a two-week long simulation game in which the class is divided into six groups of thirty students each. Each group of thirty students is then divided into six sub groups of five students each. Five of these sub groups assume the role of members of a State Department team advocating that a particular country (assigned to them from a list of twenty) should be targeted through programs to promote democracy in that country. The remaining five students play the role of the Presidential team that will be prioritizing the proposals for the President.

Schedule for the two weeks of the exercise:
- Week One
    Monday
        Large group meeting to introduce the assignment, provide context, and cover the logistics
    Wednesday
        Mandatory meeting of Presidential teams to create and finalize the evaluation rubrics. No on-site meeting scheduled for State Department teams but they are encouraged to meet physically or virtually.
    Friday
        Mandatory meeting of the State Department Teams with draft of presentation posted on LMS by 5 p.m.
- Week Two
    Monday, Wednesday, and Friday
        Two groups of thirty students meet each day to conduct the hearings in which the State Department teams present their proposals and the Presidential teams provide initial feedback. Each team is given seven minutes for the presentation and three minutes to respond to the other proposals.

Figure 5 Revised Experiential Learning Activity

The background and framework for this simulation game is provided online and through carefully selected readings. While students can find materials on their own, most Faculty Fellows believe that the introductory nature of their course and the time constraints of the exercises, dictate that the majority of the support materials be provided to the students. Each team uses a wiki to develop their presentation.

In addition to the Faculty Fellows, the monthly meetings are attended by support staff and by special invitees including Provost Office staff, the student government Advisory Board representative, and faculty leaders. See http://NGen.unt.edu/go/BookMaterials for a sample NGen monthly meeting agenda.

Presentations to internal and external audiences

Throughout the year, NGen staff, Faculty Fellows, and students present to a variety of constituencies. Within UNT, these include the academic advisors, department chair council, council of deans, council of associate deans, senior administrators, board of regents, and others. The NGen staff request a time slot at the official meetings of these groups at least once a year as well as arranging for special presentations to selected university leaders. There are also several NGen Forums each year that are open to the entire university community. The purpose of these presentations is both informational and inspirational and includes a demonstration of an NGen course by a Senior Faculty Fellow. Senior Faculty Fellows and NGen staff are encouraged to present on their NGen experience outside UNT and the Next Generation Course Redesign™ has been presented in state, regional, national and international venues each year.

In addition to presenting and publishing about their NGen experience, Faculty Fellows are strongly encouraged do provide information about their course redesign through the "snapshot" section of the NGen Web site. This snapshot of the course redesign evolves over the two years of the official NGen experience and includes information on the following:

- Student Learning Outcomes
- Assessment Plan
- Example of an Online Activity
- Example of Experiential Learning
- Report on Assessment Results
- Link to the Blog

> ### N-Gen Course Redesign
>
> HOME
>
> #### Redesign is creative work
>
> February 20, 2009
>
> As Dr. Turner said in his last post about the February meeting, this is an intensely creative time in the course redesign process. Once again, I am stepping back from the traditional approaches and allowing myself to be inventive about different, more effective ways to present the material. In fact, it is instructive to be working with a couple of graduate student teaching fellows on the redesign of the World Lit II course. First, they write a short plot-oriented quiz and a set of discussion questions for each particular text to be included on the syllabus as a learning module. This work, of course, is exactly what an instructor might do for a lecture class. The difference is that I then turn the discussion questions into either an online learning activity or an experiential face-to-face activity. For example, instead of simply posing the questions, "What is a paradox, and what parts of this text seem paradoxical?" to students, we are creating an online interactive based on an event that happens in the plot: in the story, a character sees an archway in his dream with a paradoxical

Figure 6 Sample Blog

The last item is a link to the NGen Blog where all the members of the NGen CoP are encouraged to document their redesign journey. See Figure 6 for a sample blog by NGen Faculty Fellow Dr. Tracey Gau.

Formal and informal training

In addition to the training that takes place during the retreats and monthly meetings, faculty fellows are required to attend the following four workshops in order:

1. Developing Outcomes Based Assessments (Must be taken within the first three weeks of starting the redesign process.) Participants learn how to write measurable Student Learning Outcomes and develop test plans.

2. Writing and Validating Test Items (Must be taken within the first three weeks of starting the redesign process.) Participants are provided rules, guidelines, and procedures for developing high-quality selected-response and constructed-response test items and for validating those items.
3. Writing Multiple-choice Items that Measure Higher Level Cognitive Skills (Must be taken by the middle of the second semester of the initial course redesign year.) Participants learn how to develop test items and test itemsets that include prompts to measure higher level cognitive skills.
4. Evaluating Students, Courses, and Programs (Must be taken by the end of the second semester of the initial course redesign year.) Participants are shown methods for evaluating students, courses, and programs including the use of goal attainment methodology for reporting group level attainment of learning outcomes and linking the course level to the program level.

In addition to the formal training provided, the Faculty Fellows are encouraged to meet individually with members of the Community of Practice. As an example, each Faculty Fellow meets individually with the assessment and measurement specialist, with instructional consultants, and with other support staff.

The NGen Course

As each new group of faculty fellows begins the NGen course redesign process, we challenge them to bring their creativity to their redesign. Though they are shown many examples of successful NGen courses, they are told that no two NGen courses should be alike. Each is the product of the faculty member's experience, knowledge of content, and understanding of their students. This creativity is guided by the goals of the NGen project and informed by research on learning.

Goals of NGen courses

Each NGen course strives to:

- Target higher level learning Student Learning Outcomes
- Emphasize deep versus surface learning
- Increase student engagement
- Promote cognitive development
- Enable students to learn in a challenging and diverse environment

- Develop a positive attitude toward the academic subject
- Be delivered at the same or lower cost per student as the "traditional" course

Characteristics of an NGen course

In order to meet these goals, each course that is designated as NGen is expected to contain specific attributes. These attributes were selected based on research in learning as well as on five years of course redesign experience. While specifying the characteristics expected in an NGen course provides guidelines for faculty fellows, there is considerable flexibility for creativity and inspiration to be brought to the design process. We have found that without a clear understanding of the attributes expected in an NGen course, surface rather than transformative redesign takes place and the resources invested in the redesign are wasted. Each faculty fellow is constantly challenged to describe how their redesigned course differs from its predecessor and, by the end of the redesign year, they should be able to describe how each of the following characteristics are evident in the redesign.

Carefully-crafted Student Learning Outcomes that include higher level learning

The first year of the redesign process begins with a charge to each Faculty Fellow to examine the SLO's for their course and the faculty are provided with training on creating concept maps and creating SLO's at all levels of learning. The training and examples provided especially target higher level learning and critical thinking. This is a particularly challenging area because most of the redesign faculty have little or no experience with creating quality SLO's, especially at higher levels of cognitive difficulty. The redesign faculty are encouraged to link course learning outcomes with departmental, and institutional outcomes and goals.

Faculty Fellows often enter the redesign process thinking that they know exactly what their final redesign will look like. It is important to point out to them that the SLO's can and will impact the specific instructional approaches selected and creation of SLO's is an important first step. While SLO's are a challenge, we have found that, without exception, redesign faculty acknowledge the usefulness and power of well-crafted SLO's. See Figure 7 for an example of outcomes for World Literature I.

Sample Goals and SLO's for World Literature Lesson

Institutional Goals	Departmental Goals (common to all sections of World Lit)	SLO's for the section
1. Demonstrate an awareness and recognition of the scope and variety of works of literature	1.1 Recall and recognize the historical sequence of major literary figures, texts, and movements within the Ancient, Middle, and Renaissance periods 1.2 Identify conventional literary genres, elements, and devices 1.3 Employ discipline specific vocabulary in order to recognize the relationship between form and content 1.4 Relate literary or cultural concepts, principles, terms, strategies, and styles to a range of literature	Ex.1 Recognize that the history of representative epics are oral or written compositions Ex.2 Identify major characters and figures that appear in more than one text Ex. 3 Apply genre characteristics to representative texts Ex.4 Identify and connect literary or cultural concepts as they directly relate to representative texts
2. Read critically and analytically	2.1 Analyze, evaluate, interpret, synthesize representative texts from the Eastern and Western traditions and relate them to their literary and cultural contexts 2.2 Compare and contrast major literary figures, their situations, decisions 2.3 Make connections among various periods, texts, authors, and characters 2.4 Evaluate the ideas presented in a text, their implications, and their relationship to ideas beyond the text	Ex.5 Relate cultural qualities of a hero to a representative character Ex.6 Compare the Eastern depiction of fate, virtue, and heroism to the Western depiction in representative texts Ex.7 Differentiate between concepts, such as absolutism and relativism, using examples from representative texts Ex.8 Evaluate characters' decisions and actions in the context of their various cultures and worldviews

© Dr. Tracey Gau Reprinted with permission

Figure 7 Sample Outcomes in World Literature I

An assessment plan with test items

Success rates as defined by course grades continue to be the most visible and sensitive benchmark in higher education. While the percentage of students earning a "C" or above and particularly the cost per each of those "successful" students is tracked as part of the evaluation process, the most important indicator of success is whether students meet the SLO's for the course. Each NGen course maps a student learning outcome to multiple choice test items at various difficulty and to a constructed response test item. For the latter, faculty prepare a scoring rubric.

As with SLO's, creating an assessment plan with valid and reliable test items is often breaking new ground with redesign faculty. Again, training, many examples, and much encouragement are provided by an assessment and measurement specialist and others. The first three months of the redesign year are devoted to review, creation, and assessment of the SLO's. This is hard work and the redesign faculty often want to get to the "fun stuff" but we remind them that they need to, "eat their vegetables before they get dessert", and most realize the importance of establish this good foundation for their redesign. See Figure 8 for an example of a portion of an assessment plan with sample test items.

Sample Test Items for SLO Ex 5: Relate Cultural Qualities of a Hero to a Representative Character

- Multiple Choice Items (**Correct Responses in Bold**)

    Low Difficulty Level Item

    1. According to Machiavelli, what two animals must a ruler imitate and what meaning does the analogy represent?
        a. Fox and Tiger; in addition to being cunning, a ruler must protect himself from traps
        b. Fox and Cougar, in addition to being cunning, a ruler must be able to act alone
        c. **Fox and Lion; in addition to being cunning, a ruler must use force as well as laws to rule**

    Medium Difficulty Level Item

    1. Which piece of evidence that Iago presents to Othello has the greatest effect of conjuring up doubt about Desdemona's fidelity?
        a. Cassio's erotic dream
        b. Cassio's drunken brawl with Roderigo
        c. **The handkerchief he sees Cassio give to Bianca**

    High Difficulty Level Item

    1. What is the BEST interpretation of Iago's advice to Roderigo to "put money in thy purse"?
        a. **Invest your time, money, and effort in joining Iago in revenge against Othello**
        b. The marriage between Desdemona and Othello is frail and can easily be broken
        c. Because of woman's changeable nature, Desdemona will tire of Othello and seek a new lover

- Constructed Response Items

    1. Demonstrate how the concept of virtue gets redefined in the Renaissance. Compare the Renaissance understanding of virtue to how it was understood and defined in the Ancient and Middle periods. Give examples for each.
    2. Define the term *Machiavellianism* and apply it to any character from any of the representative Renaissance texts.

    © Dr. Tracey Gau Reprinted with permission

Figure 8 Portion of Assessment Plan

A research-based blend of instructional approaches

Higher level Student Learning Outcomes and a first-rate assessment plan are important characteristics of an NGen course. However, they are just the start of the course redesign and the real creativity comes in creating a combination of in-class and online instructional experiences that will enable the students to reach the SLO's. To be designated as an NGen course, the combination of large group, online, and small group activities should each fall within a suggested range of percentages of contact hour delivery (See Figure 9).

These percentages are presented as guidelines to the Faculty Fellows as they redesign their courses. While there are many examples of high-quality general education courses that do not fit this model, the combination recommended in the NGen approach is based on current brain research and increases the probability that students will be engaged in deep learning. Each of the three NGen course elements brings specific strengths to the instructional process.

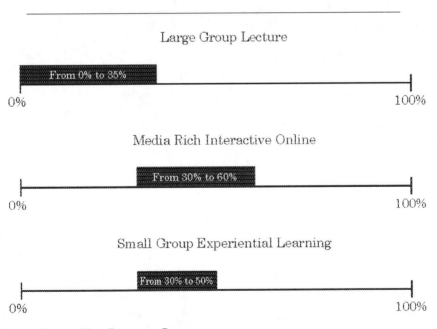

Figure 9 Contact Hour Percentage Range

The lecture is best used to:

- Create interest and motivation and provide assurance that the students can be successful
- Clarify and expand upon rather than deliver content
- Model the acquisition of knowledge that is idiosyncratic to that field, e.g. how does a historian/chemist/sociologist approach a research question?
- Present critical concrete and lower level concepts to scaffold learning for the most difficult higher level concepts

The online environment is best used to:

- Acquire lower level learning to free up time for in-class experiential learning
- Chunk content to overcome working memory limits
- Provide low-stakes assessments, such as quizzes, for practice and confidence building
- Provide psychomotor experiences such as drag and drop exercises
- Provide concrete experiences that are guided and efficient

Experiential learning can range from simple group projects to true problem-based learning (PBL). This strategy is best used to:

- Introduce an emotional component
- Analyze, evaluate, and synthesize information
- Present and defend newly acquired hypotheses
- Provide collaborative, cooperative, and academic controversy activities that encourage thinking critically from multiple perspectives

Conclusion

The Next Generation Course Redesign™ Project has evolved over the years into an efficient process that results in a general education course redesigned for high levels of student engagement and deep learning. The redesign process brings together an expanding Community of Practice that supports and enables Faculty Fellows through two years of redesign. These fellows emerge with a redesigned and proven course and with the skills to assume a leadership position in course redesign within their department, the university, and beyond.

· CHAPTER FOUR ·

OUTCOME BASED ASSESSMENT AND COURSE REDESIGN

Provides information on the various methods that the NGen Project utilizes for assessment of student learning as well as for determining the impact of the project itself.

A major component of course redesign is the development of learning outcomes that are measurable and the development of assessments that contain items that match the outcomes. This often appears to be a daunting task for faculty who have little or no previous training in assessment and measurement. They are relieved to find that throughout the NGen redesign training process, it is emphasized that much of what is needed for the outcome-assessment component of their redesign may already exist in some form in the materials that the faculty members are currently using. There is typically no need to start from scratch. NGen redesign faculty receive eight hours of formal outcome based assessment training and receive additional training at monthly meetings where they share their redesign progress. They can meet with an assessment and measurement specialist as needed. The following four steps present an overview of the outcome based assessment process used for the NGen redesign model.

Step 1: Developing the Outcome Statements

Outcomes and Assessment Defined

Assessment is broadly defined for the NGen redesign program as any process or procedure that is used to obtain information about students and student learning. Student learning outcomes (SLOs) are statements that tell what students are expected to know and be able to do. Results from outcome based assessments are used to evaluate the success of the student in meeting the SLOs and to assign some type of indicator of success (such as a grade). Assessment results are also used to evaluate the effectiveness of a particular instructor's course redesign and additionally to evaluate the worth of the NGen course redesign program. Assessments typically fall into the following categories: cognitive tests that are used to measure knowledge and skills, and affective tests that are used to measure student attitude and opinion.

SLOs and measurability

The NGen redesign program requires faculty members to be well trained in writing SLOs that are clear, reasonable, fair, and measurable. For NGen faculty, SLO measurability simply means that what the SLO states can be observed and measured in some reasonable, fair, and feasible way. For some purposes it is best to measure with selected response test formats, such as multiple-choice items. For other purposes, it is best to measure with constructed-response test-items, such as writing short answers, writing answers that may be a paragraph or more, or writing extended responses that may be several pages or a long report. In other circumstances it may be best to measure a student performance, such as a dance or musical performance (keep in mind that a written response could also be considered a "performance").

The goal-outcome hierarchy

NGen redesign faculty are required to utilize a particular hierarchy when developing outcome statements. This hierarchy starts with an overall Goal that describes what is expected of a student at the broadest outcome level. In other words, the course goals provide a description of the expectations for a student to be successful. A Goal may also be called an Objective or an Overall Outcome. Typically, three or more of these Goal\Objective\Overall-outcome statements are needed to cover the course content, but there is not a specific limit to the number of goals, other than what can reasonably be covered in a semester.

Here is an example of a Goal: Goal 1, *The student will demonstrate an understanding of the facts and chronology of United States history.*

The Goal statement, in almost all cases, is too broad to know exactly what type of items or item formats should be written to measure it, so the next step is to break the Goal into smaller, more measurable outcomes. This middle level of the NGen outcome hierarchy is labeled the General Outcome (GO) level. There should be at least two GOs for a particular Goal, and typically there will be three or more. The following is a possible GO under Goal 1 above: GO 1.1, The *student will connect and evaluate causal and consequential factors of main events in United States History.*

These GOs are very helpful for communicating to the students more specifically what they are expected to know and be able to do, and they work well as a component in a syllabus, but more specificity is needed in order to know what items to write. Item writing shouldn't be a guessing game about what the item might be. The item, in essence, should "fall out" of the outcome statement. In other words, the outcome needs to be so specific that there is no question about what needs to be measured. Thus, we move to the final and most specific level of the outcome hierarchy, to the Specific Learning Outcome (SLO) level. The letters SLO are used generally in the literature to mean Student Learning Outcome, but in the NGen outcome hierarchy, they mean Specific Learning Outcome. The following is an example of an SLO that could go under GO 1.1 above: SLO 1.1.1, The *student can explain the causes of Reconstruction in the South.*

Possible sources for Goals, GO's and SLO's

Throughout the outcome and test development process, NGen redesign faculty are reminded that much of what is needed for the assessment component of their course redesign probably already exists in some form in their current syllabi and course materials. It is often the case that broader outcomes and goals exist in some form in the course materials, and they can be refined and broken down into smaller more measurable statements. Curriculum maps that lay out what is to be covered for the course can be used to identify gaps, duplications, overage, and missing content that need to be addressed with outcome statements.

NGen redesign faculty are reminded that they are experts in their content area and that they redesign their outcomes and student assessments for the following purposes:

- To document clearly and exactly what needs to be taught and learned so that the instructor and the students can be on the same page in terms of requirements and expectations.
- To determine the depth and breadth of what needs to be taught so that the instructor knows what can reasonably be covered in the time allotted

- To determine the degree to which deep learning versus surface learning of the course material is expected
- To determine the number, difficulty, and types of test items that are needed in order to have the information needed to make a valid inference about student learning and to fairly assess the student's learning
- To have clear and measurable outcome statements so that test items can be developed that match the content and intent of the outcomes
- To be able to track student progress in accomplishing the learning outcomes through formative assessments that directly related to the outcomes
- To be able to develop fair and reasonable summative assessments for assigning student grades

Step 2: Developing the Test Specifications Plan

Following the development of measurable outcomes, NGen redesign faculty are guided through the process of creating test specifications. Test specifications are the most important component of a test plan. The purpose of the test specifications is to lay out how many and what type of items are needed to make the tests that will be used to determine the degree to which students have achieved the learning outcomes. Other parts of a test plan include such information as whether a test is to be used to obtain formative information or summative information, whether the same items will be randomized on forms for security reasons, and whether there should be a pretest-posttest administration. Tables of test specifications can vary in format depending on the particular needs for a course, but the following elements typically need to be addressed:

1. Each Goal that is being measured.
2. The GOs under the Goals that are being measured.
3. The SLOS under the GOs that are being measured.
4. The number of items that will be used to measure each of the SLOs.
5. The types of items that will be used (selected response and\or constructed response)
6. The difficulty level of the items (Low, Medium, or High.)

7. In the case of constructed response, whether the response is to be a short statement, a paragraph, or an extended response of one or many pages.

Step 3: Writing and Validating Test Items

Once the outcomes are developed and the test plan and test specifications are developed, the NGen re-designer has a clear picture of what the student needs to know and should be able to do, how many and what type of items may be needed, and the difficulty level of the items. Next, the items need to be written.

Item writing rules and guidelines for selected response and constructed response items

NGen redesign faculty are trained in item writing. Space does not allow for a listing here of the many rules and guidelines for writing selected (e.g. multiple-choice) response items and for constructed (written) response items, but excellent coverage can be found in texts by Osterlind (1998), Haladyna (1999), and Carriveau (2008). Examples of multiple-choice item writing guidelines are:

- There should be only one clearly correct answer.
- The correct answer should not be clued by the question.
- Negatives should be avoided except where absolutely necessary.

Examples of constructed-response item writing guidelines include:

- The outcomes addressed should correlate with the length of the response expected
- The prompt should contain all the information the student needs in order to understand the task.
- The question should contain all the information the student needs.

Test score validity

A common statement by faculty is that the test needs to be valid. Technically, validity is a property of the scores produced by the test, not the test form itself. In other words, the concern is the degree to which the test scores can be used and interpreted for what they were intended to measure. For example, scores from a test that was designed to measure a student's knowledge of periods of art history would lack validity for measuring the student's ability to analyze one particular artist's style and technique. NGen redesign faculty are trained to make sure there is a match between the outcomes statement and the items.

Validating selected response test items

For NGen redesign faculty, the validation of their selected response consists of two major components. First, the faculty member must validate that the test items directly measure what the outcomes state. This is primarily a content and intent issue. For example, if the content of the item matches the content of the outcome statement, then this is a piece of validity evidence to support the use of the test score for its intended purpose.

Second, an item analysis must be conducted in which the percentage of students responding to each option (answer choice) of each items is examined. After instruction, it could be expected that students would score reasonably well on a particular test item. If items were designated as a high difficulty item in the test specifications, then the number of students getting the item correct would be less than for an item that was designated as a low difficulty item. Any item that doesn't function as expected needs to be examined to determine what may have caused this to occur. Adjustments must then be made as needed.

Additionally, the item analysis contains information that helps to determine the degree to which an item discriminates between low scoring students and high scoring students. If the students who are in the highest scoring group (usually the top 27%) score very low on a particular item that students in the lowest scoring group (the lowest 27%) score very high on, then this item needs to be examined to determine what may have caused this to occur and then make adjustments as needed. Where possible, the newly developed items and test forms are field tested to determine how well the items are functioning and to decide whether to keep, modify, or delete an item. Once the items are determined to be acceptable, they are used for regular testing, but an item analysis should still be conducted because validating items is an ongoing process.

Validating constructed response test items

Just like selected response items, constructed response items need to undergo validity testing. Because constructed responses from students are scored with a scoring rubric, the outcomes that are being tested need to be included in the scoring rubric. That is, like selected response items, the first piece of validity evidence is that the content being measured by the rubric is directly matched to the outcomes and is clearly stated.

A second piece of validity evidence for constructed response items is the degree to which the prompt and the question generates responses that were expected. If the length of the response and the information provided was generally much less than expected, then the prompt and question may need revision. If many of the student responses were off topic, then the prompt and question likely needs revision. The purpose of a well-crafted constructed response item is to generate enough response from students to be able to determine the degree to which the students meet the outcome expectations.

A third piece of validity evidence when using constructed response items is the distribution of scores along the scale that is used to assign the scores. For example, if a four point scale is used with 4 being the best response and 1 being the poorest response, then it is easy to analyze in which categories the students did better or worse. This analysis, of course, provides some diagnostic information, but it also needs to be considered in terms of what the expectations and discriminations among high and low scoring students are. For example, if one of the outcomes being measured shows a lot of low scores for students who have overall high scores and high scores for students who have overall low scores, then this particular outcome item is not discriminating well between low ability and high ability students.

Step 4: Evaluating Redesigned Courses and Programs

N-Gen redesign faculty use both cognitive and affective test instruments to obtain information about the success of their students and the success of their redesign. Additionally, the results are used to evaluate the NGen program. The assessments described below are provided as examples of what may be used to gather useful information about student, course, and program success.

Preference for course format

The *Preference for Course Format Survey* is administered at the end of each semester and asks the students which instructional format they would choose if they were to take the course over again, the redesigned N-Gen format or the traditional face-to-face format. Then the student is asked to write a short written response in which the student explains the reason(s) for his\her choice. At the end of the course, the instructor records an S for successful (student received an A, B, or C) and a U for un-successful (student received a D,F,W, or I) next to each student's format preference, which allows for comparisons of successful and unsuccessful students, to their format preference. This information is important for validity evidence for the particular course redesign and for the NGen redesign program.

Student attitude toward subject of the course

The *Survey of Student Attitude Toward Subject of the Course* is designed to gather information on how the student feels about the subject matter of the course. It is not intended to measure the instructor's effectiveness or the course effectiveness. There are twenty-one items on this survey on a five point scale from Strongly Disagree to Strongly Agree. This survey is administered at the beginning of the course and at the end of the course and the differences are tested for significance. This type of information is important to the instructor in terms of increasing student appreciation for the subject matter and also provides validity evidence for supporting the course redesign. The survey was adapted, with permission from, Pearcy, A.G. (2008). Finding the perfect blend: A comparative study of face-to-face, online, and blended instruction. Unpublished doctoral dissertation. University of North Texas.

Learning Environment Preferences (LEP) survey

The LEP (Moore, W. S., 1990) is five one-page surveys, each containing 13 items plus 3 summary items each. The survey is designed to measure patterns of longitudinal intellectual development across various subgroups of students or for pre-post evaluations of specific courses or groups of courses. A general Cognitive Complexity Index (CCI) is obtained that measures intellectual development on a scale of 200–500. Additionally, and of what is also of interest to N-gen courses, are four separate category scores that indicate the type of learning environment the student prefers. These category scores can be used to study the match of what type of environment the student prefers to what the instructor perceives the environment to be. A pre-post change per course would be good information to inform continued course redesign. A pre only assessment would provide insights into preferences that may be used to modify a course redesign going into the semester. A post only could be used to evaluate the course redesign over time. The LEP is used to address the NGen redesign goal to include higher level cognitive tasks (critical thinking and evaluative skills) in the course redesign.

Final score distribution

NGen redesign faculty compare their pre-NGen end of course score distributions to their post-NGen redesign final score distributions to see if there are differences. Then they compare the NGen redesign course distributions from semester to semester. Increases in the number of students who pass and the number of students who are in the higher grade categories are an indication of a successful redesign. Increased student success is the goal of the redesign program. Shifts in grade categories can be used to make informed decisions for ongoing course redesign. For example, the instructor may consider that having outcomes and test items that address higher cognitive tasks raises the quality of the course but also may have an effect on those students who struggle with these types of tasks. The instructor would then consider instructional strategies in the redesign to address this effect.

Outcome attainment values

NGen redesign faculty are also concerned with the degree to which the class as a whole met the specific learning outcomes. In other words, a measure of outcome attainment is needed. In an NGen redesign course, there is a clear match between the test item (whether selected response or constructed response) and the specific learning outcome. Thus, the percentage of students who got each test item correct or met the criteria for the particular outcomes measured on a scoring rubric can be computed and matched to a particular specific learning outcome. The percentages for a set of items that measure a particular outcome can then be averaged, and this average becomes the outcome attainment value for the particular specific learning outcome. For example, if there are four items that measure specific learning outcome 1.2.1 and the average percentage for the four items is .80, then it can be said that the outcome attainment for the class for that particular outcome is .80. This type of information gives the instructor more diagnostic information on student achievement of the outcomes than is provided by grade distributions.

Surveys used to gather information for evaluation of the NGen program

Survey of Course Evaluation by Instructor Who Designed and Taught the Course

This survey is designed to address the perceptions of self efficacy, attitudes, barriers, and behaviors around the use of the redesigned course. The survey contains a few demographic items followed by 5 items on a 5 point scale from Strongly Disagree to Strongly Agree.

Survey of Course Evaluation by Instructor Who Taught the Course But Did Not Design It

This survey is designed to address the perceptions of self efficacy, attitudes, barriers, and behaviors around the use of the redesigned course when the user did not design the course. The survey contains a few demographic items followed by 6 items on a 5 point scale from Strongly Disagree to Strongly Agree.

Survey of Course Evaluation by Department Chairs and Deans of Redesigned Courses

This survey is designed to address the perceptions of self efficacy, attitudes, barriers, and behaviors around the use of the redesigned course as perceived by chairs and deans in which an NGen course is being taught in their department and college. The survey contains a few demographic items followed by 7 items on a 5 point scale from Strongly Disagree to Strongly Agree.

Adoption of Courseware Survey for Faculty Members

This survey is administered to faculty in general and specifically to faculty in departments that house a redesigned course to determine the degree to which barriers to the sharing of courseware are perceived. The target population is those faculty who are not using an NGen redesigned course. This survey asks for some demographic information followed by 23 items on a five point scale.

Community of Practice Survey

Developing a strong community of practicing NGen faculty and sustaining the community is one of the goals of the NGen program. The *Community of Practice* (CoP) *Survey* is used to gather data on the amount and quality of interaction with\among members of the NGen community. Part 1 of the survey measures four dimensions: frequency of contacts, responsiveness to the contact, effectiveness of the response, and the enthusiasm or energy level of the contact. Part 2 of the survey has 26 statements, each on a scale of 1–5, and measures CoP member opinions on the organizational context in which the QEP operates. The information obtained from the CoP is used as an indication of the sustainability of the NGen program.

The surveys described above are modified as needed to meet the needs of the NGen course redesign program. They are presented here primarily to demonstrate the breadth of the information utilized in the NGen process for making informed decisions about course redesign and student learning. Other institutions may find that they need different or additional information.

Conclusion

This chapter has presented an overview of the outcome, assessment, and evaluation components of an NGen course redesign. When redesigning a course to fit the NGen model, these components are as essential as the instructional strategies and courseware that are developed. In order to have valid results and information for making instructional decisions, it must be shown that the assessments match the outcomes and that the instruction and courseware used match the outcomes. In other words, the outcomes describe *what* is to be learned, the instructional model and courseware are *how* the students will interact in a learning environment to obtain success with the *what*, and the assessments are the measuring devices to determine the degree to which the students are learning or have learned the *what*. NGen redesign faculty accept this model and learn to apply it successfully.

· CHAPTER FIVE ·

ENABLING COURSE REDESIGN

The information in this chapter is intended to provide the foundation for successful and sustained course redesign projects. Guidelines for identifying the problem, planning, marshalling support, identifying effective leadership, and creating and sustaining the course redesign team are provided. Special challenges engendered by the nontraditional space and time requirements of redesigned courses are addressed, as well as the changes to the current faculty reward system.

Barriers to Course Redesign

As discussed in Chapter One, widespread and sustainable change is difficult within an institution that has existed unchanged at its core for hundreds of years. The power and authority within institutions of higher education are diffused and administrators face myriad demands. Faculty spend most of their time laboring in a "culture of emptiness" (Lee, Hyman, and Luginbuhl, 2007) within a climate that values individuality and freedom of choice and includes little accountability for teaching effectiveness.

The reward system is often skewed toward research, especially research that is externally funded. The most prestigious teaching is often at the graduate and upper division levels. General education courses are often assigned to graduate students, "day labor" adjuncts, out-of-favor senior faculty, and instructors, many of whom are teaching while seeking "real" academic positions.

Classroom design and furnishings make any approach other than lecture a challenge. In addition, "slot-based" classroom scheduling and inflexible registration systems make experimenting with flexible use of facilities difficult.

Guidelines for a Successful Course Redesign Process

Even with these barriers, there are compelling reasons to undertake the transformation of general education courses and powerful tools to use in this transformation. The following guidelines are meant to be more informative than prescriptive, as every institution differs in its culture, faculty, students, and the resources that it can bring to bear.

Identify the problem and propose the solution (carefully)

What is it that you are trying to fix? What is the evidence that it is broken? Course redesign should not be another educational reform "solution" that is imposed without carefully collecting data so that limited resources can be allocated to the courses that are in most need of redesign. Often the assessment process that generates the information required for these decisions needs to be created as part of the redesign process.

Even without a high-quality learning assessment process in place, it is possible to collect data on completion and success rates for the courses considered as well as the rates from upper division courses for which the general education courses are required. If there are significant numbers of general education classes in which 30% or more of the students do not succeed, this can serve as a trigger for course redesign.

Whatever method is used to identify the problem, if it is determined that a course redesign project is the solution of choice, it is important that this solution be proposed positively. Thirty percent or more of the students in a course not succeeding *is* a problem, but initiating a course redesign effort by assigning blame only serves to put faculty on the defensive. Such pushback by faculty is exemplified by Mattson (2005), who expresses resentment as being portrayed as 'not caring' and questions why already overloaded faculty are being asked to fix large classes instead of the administration putting resources into reducing class size.

If certain general education classes seem to be good candidates for redesign, the challenge is to collect data that will buttress the argument and identify the highest priority courses. One must walk a fine line between urgency and alarm in proposing course redesign. This balance is important not only in bringing faculty on board but also in publicizing the project externally. Course redesign can be about making good instruction better.

Select the right leader

As with any major project, leadership is crucial. While there will be many players in a successful redesign project, there needs to be one person who is responsible for leading the effort. This person should be appointed by, report to, and have regular access to the chief academic officer.

Leading the course redesign effort should be the primary responsibility, major focus, and passion of the project leader. Ideally, they should have extensive teaching as well as academic administrative experience. The project leader will need to be able to communicate successfully with all constituents in the institution.

Plan for the long term

Substantive transformative change involves thousands of decisions by hundreds of faculty and such change does not occur overnight. Short-term projects often create pockets of innovation that ultimately die out. For change to develop, be nurtured, and have a chance to be sustained after the official project ends, a multi-year effort should be pursued.

During the years of the project, it is likely that changes will occur in the upper administration. In the first five years of UNT's course redesign project, we had two presidents and three provosts! It is important that at the onset of the course redesign project, a long range plan exists with funding projected throughout the project's life. Of course, there are no ironclad guarantees in higher education, and the project leader will need to convince and assure new presidents and provosts of the impact and worth of continuing the redesign project.

Decide whether to target a single department or an entire institution

The project's scope is one of the most important decisions in course redesign. This decision should be guided by need, but the impetus can come from an individual department or from several departments. The advantage of targeting a single department is that the department is the basic academic and administrative unit in the institution and making the necessary changes to incentives, scheduling, space utilization, and other infrastructure support in one department rather than across the institution will be easier. In addition, a redesign team all from one discipline will increase the probability that team members will relate to each other and recognize the validity of each other's experiences. The redesign team can also provide mutual support in the attempt to replicate the redesign to other sections of the course and across other courses in the department. Lee, Hyman, and Luginbuhl (2007) provide valuable advice in department-based course redesign.

While there are good reasons for using the academic department as the primary area of operations for a course redesign effort, there are drawbacks to this approach. If the ultimate goal is to impact teaching and learning throughout the institution, limiting the project to one department each year may take too much time and the potential for an innovation "silo" is high. In addition, it may be difficult to garner and maintain the support of senior administration or faculty leadership without an immediate multi-department impact. It is also unlikely that faculty teaching general education courses in departments not involved will jump the "discipline divide" and redesign their course without the support provided by the redesign project.

A different approach to course design would be to create a cohort of courses from a variety of disciplines by designating certain criteria for inclusion. As an example, these criteria might include an enrollment of at least 100 students in a section and success rates less than 75%. The advantage of a multidisciplinary approach is the potential of immediate institution-wide impact and the perception of ownership by the entire academic community. In addition, sharing course redesign with faculty from other disciplines can be informative as well as exhilarating. As an example, the NGen World Literature II redesign team came up with the idea of students creating Facebook™-type pages for characters in literature and the Organic Chemistry instructor adapted this idea by designing an activity in which students create a virtual 'personal space' for organic molecules.

Of course, there are potential problems with an interdisciplinary approach. Since usually only one or two faculty from a department are involved, they may not represent a critical mass for change within the group of instructors who teach all of the sections of the course. The innovating faculty can be shunned and punished no matter how effective the redesign. Therefore, it is important if the interdisciplinary approach is followed, to work with department chairs and other gatekeepers within the department to provide protection for the innovating faculty.

Decide whether to redesign a single section or every section of the course

Another planning decision to determine is whether to redesign a single section with the goal of sustaining and replicating the design across other sections of the course or to employ an "all or nothing" approach that involves a commitment to redesign every section of the course at once. The single section approach is simpler and requires only one instructor willing to participate in redesign, but replication of the redesign can be a challenge. However, requiring a commitment to redesign all sections before the course redesign has begun may be a tough sell and is unlikely to occur often in any given institution.

In creating the long range plan, you might also want to consider "low stakes" redesign opportunities in addition to providing for the redesign of an entire course. These can involve the redesign of a single unit of a course or even a portion of a single day's lesson. Such projects provide the opportunity for training and recruiting future participants in the full course redesign project. See http://NGen.unt.edu/go/BookMaterials for examples of UNT's Transformative Instructional Initiative Project.

Whatever approach is taken to the course resign, the long range plan must contain elements that will sustain the change as it occurs and support replication of the redesign. If an interdisciplinary approach is used, the plan should contain activities that encourage the continued use of the redesigned course as well as the adoption and adaption of the redesign in additional sections. If the initial redesign is limited to a department, the long range plan needs to contain actions that will sustain and expand the project within the department as well as encourage additional departments to adopt course redesign.

Plan for the short term

While recognizing that many of the elements of a course redesign project can and should evolve over the long term, it is very important to create a detailed calendar for the first year or two of the project. (See http://NGen.unt.edu/go/BookMaterials for a sample two-year course redesign calendar.)

Activities on this planning calendar might include:

- Soliciting involvement by faculty (RFP or invitation letters)
- Creating project Web site
- Identifying and selecting key support personnel
- Selecting courses to be redesigned for the year
- Regular and extended (retreats) meetings for the redesign faculty and support staff
- Campus-wide events such as forums

- Information sessions for targeted groups such as student government, faculty senate, and academic advisors
- Selection of mentor faculty

The detailed short-range plan should include assessment activities for data gathering. As an example, "January 15-Februrary 1, administer Attitude Toward Subject Survey." Finally, the plan should include activities that assess and measure the redesign process, including target dates for reporting to constituents such as the chief academic officer, advisory board, and faculty senate.

Obtain support at all levels of the institution

Understanding of and support for the redesign effort throughout the institution is crucial. The project needs to be in the president's "cocktail party" speech, i.e., when they speak or write about the institution's accomplishments or exciting plans, the redesign project needs to be on the list. While the chief academic officer's understanding and ownership of the redesign project is crucial, the support of every senior administrator is also important. As an example, the course redesign project activities must be integrated and symbiotic with student development activities. Continued positive publicity both inside and outside the institution is important. The positive impact on students from diverse backgrounds needs to be understood. Scheduling and space issues need to be resolved and information technology support is critical.

Of course, the chief financial officer needs to understand that investments in course redesign make good financial as well as academic sense. Assessment activities should include cost per successful and highly successful student as one output. This is important because a transformative institution-wide course redesign project requires an upfront and ongoing financial commitment. Depending on the existing infrastructure, new money for a project director, assessment specialist, instructional consultants, faculty grants, office assistance, and operating might have to be found and allocated. The probability of these resources being allocated and continued will be increased by positive assessment results.

Planning for and funding the technology support infrastructure is also critical. Most course redesigns utilize Web-based delivery for at least some of the content. In the NGen approach, a media-rich interactive online environment is utilized for thirty to sixty percent of the contact hours. An important planning task is to decide how the online component of the redesign courses will be produced and supported. Will this component be limited to commercial, low cost, or no cost courseware? While the amount and quality of courseware provided by textbook publishers has increased significantly, it is still limited in breadth of topic and in depth of approach.

If the decision is made to support production of courseware on campus, the impact on existing production resources needs to be carefully considered and the priority of redesign courses in the production schedule established and agreed upon. Also ownership of learning objects, interactives, and other course redesign elements needs to be established before production begins. See http://clear.unt.edu/index2.cfm?M=15&SM=19 for a link to the University of North Texas's intellectual property policy.

Create an effective Community of Practice

Long term course redesign requires putting together and sustaining a variety of human resources. An important task is to begin with a small number of participants and add additional faculty while maintaining the involvement of the pioneers.

Bring together faculty and support staff to ensure initial success

The right redesign faculty is critical, especially for the first cohort, since their course redesigns will serve as models and they will serve as ambassadors and mentors. When the NGen staff speaks about our project, we find that the audience listens politely but often skeptically. It is when the NGen Senior Faculty Fellows describe and demonstrate their redesigned courses that the real interest becomes manifest.

Although it is tempting to utilize an invitation-only approach to selecting the redesign faculty, this does not lend itself to the atmosphere of inclusiveness that is important for the long term sustainability of the redesign project. We utilize a Request for Proposal (RFP) and encourage all faculty whose classes meet the criteria to apply. However, we do identify and encourage faculty to apply who are likely to succeed and whose courses will have a significant impact. These "high-potential" faculty are identified by:

- Reviewing class size and success rate information to identify high impact potential and contacting faculty who teach these sections, requesting to meet with them to discuss the redesign project

- Holding NGen information sessions each spring to discuss requirements for participating and to demonstrate existing redesigns
- Offering an Institution-wide forum featuring a panel of NGen Senior Faculty Fellows one month before the RFP is issued
- Using our small-scale redesign projects as a "breeding ground" for future NGen Faculty Fellows

In addition to the redesign faculty and the course redesign support staff, it is important to have the ongoing participation of student development staff, librarians, instructional consultants, courseware production staff, assessment and evaluation staff, and others whose involvement will increase the likelihood of success of the project. Of course, there can be literally hundreds of people at the institution whose support is crucial, but it is important to create and maintain a Course Redesign Community of Practice that meets regularly and serves as a source of information, knowledge, and inspiration.

Provide the necessary support

Ideally every course redesign faculty member will successfully redesign, teach, evaluate and continuously improve their course. They will receive the support they need to evolve from mentee to mentor as part of an enlarging CoP. Encouraging this requires a wide variety of support, patience, and persistence.

Provide training

Few faculty enter the redesign process with the requisite skills in creating student learning outcomes that represent all levels of cognitive learning or in creating and managing a robust assessment plan. Therefore, it is important that training in these areas be made available early and often. Other training topics for consideration include group learning, peer teaching, and the whole spectrum of mediated learning.

Provide structure

Faculty are busy and good intentions alone do not necessarily result in good course redesign. We have found that it is critical to provide benchmarks and expectations to new course redesign faculty for the upcoming two years and to constantly remind them of due dates and deliverables. We also pay grants to faculty in installments based on agreed upon goal attainment.

Structure is also important because the vast majority of faculty have been exposed to lecture-dominated instruction and this approach is deeply ingrained in their psyche. We have been surprised by Faculty Fellows who participated in many presentations of redesigned courses, and seemingly were on board with the approach and then proposed a preliminary course redesign in March that consisted of their lecturing for all of the contact hours. It is true that not every new redesign faculty has to "get it" from the onset. As Asmar (2002) points out, beliefs often follow behavior and ownership with understanding is not necessary at the start of the project as long as it is present at the end. However, a failed redesign costs too much in human and financial resources to blindly trust that each redesign faculty understands and is willing to make the radical changes necessary in their pedagogy. Therefore, we recommend documents that clearly describe what a redesigned course should look like (with ample room for creativity, of course.) (See http://NGen.unt.edu/go/BookMaterials for examples of documents that assist in structuring the redesign process.)

Provide incentives

Being part of a thriving course redesign project in itself can be a great motivator. Working with faculty that share the passion of innovation in teaching and learning is exciting. Recognition of the course redesign faculty throughout their involvement in the project can be an important incentive. Such recognition can include:

- Holding events at which the faculty are recognized (invite their department chair/dean to attend)
- Providing certificates for completing training
- Featuring course redesign faculty on the project's web site as well as in other venues (This is where a relationship with the public relations staff is important!)
- Creating "signature" clothing with the course redesign project logo and providing it to all members of the CoP
- Creating an official mentorship status for course redesign faculty who have completed a successful redesign, pilot, and revision

While these types of recognition can be effective, financial incentives are important for sustaining the project over the long term. These incentives can be in the form of grants to the faculty to provide for course release, student assistants to help research content, special equipment needs, or other ways of helping the redesign faculty succeed. Sharing the ownership of the electronically delivered portion of the course is also a possibility. It is also important to provide continuing financial incentives to faculty who stay on as active members of the CoP.

Focus relentlessly on assessment

Initially, course redesign makes for good press. The students are often involved in learning experiences that make good photo opportunities. Course redesign faculty are enthusiastic and articulate about their new way of teaching. However, sooner rather than later, someone is going to ask for results. What is the return on the investment in the course redesign project?

Since you know this is going to happen, it is important to have a robust multi-faceted assessment plan in place at the start of the redesign project. At the heart of the plan is the assessment of Student Learning Outcomes (SLOs) that represent all levels of cognition and that have been agreed upon by the faculty teaching all of the sections of the course being redesigned. Ultimately, this is the only real way of comparing the redesign to the traditional method. Of course, this is the ideal and arriving at such a consensus can take years. Most importantly, the redesign needs to include the SLO's and assessment plan for each redesigned class as its foundation.

While the drawback of comparing sections of classes based on grades (success rates) is widely recognized as problematic, such comparisons will inevitably be made since these are often the only commonly available data. Therefore, it is important to keep track of success rates of the redesign and traditional sections of a course. Make an attempt to ensure that the redesign sections do not fare poorly in comparison and be prepared to compare student learning outcomes if this happens. Other assessment points can include:

- Student preference for redesign or traditional
- Student attitude toward subject
- Student engagement
- Student cognitive development

While good assessment results can ensure that the redesign project will continue, the most important use of these results is for improving the redesign. Habituating a cycle of redesign and assessment is an important goal in any redesign project.

Get and keep the word out

Maintaining an awareness of the course redesign project throughout the academic community is important. Positive awareness will make it easier to attract the best course redesign faculty and keep administrators on board. Most importantly, continuing positive public relations can sustain the members of the CoP when they encounter the inevitable negative responses. It is naïve to expect that a radically different approach to teaching will be welcomed by everyone. In fact, pushback from faculty who see course redesign as an imposition, insult, misuse of resources, and a distraction from their main interests is inevitable. There will be students who do not want to leave the large lecture format for an approach that requires more interaction with other students, higher levels of reflection, and questions that might not have one correct answer (Inderbitzin and Storrs, 2008; A.H., Moore, Fowler, and Watson, 2007).

In publicizing the course redesign project, strive for the right mixture of urgency, enthusiasm, and transparency. Manage expectations by labeling the initial implementation of the redesign as a "pilot" and expect the implementation "dip" in outcomes the first time the redesigned course is offered. The approach to which you are comparing the redesign has had centuries of refinement and it is unrealistic to expect a redesign, with all of the complications of scheduling, technology, and new ways of learning, to be glitch-proof out of the box. Stick with the assessment plan and continuing revision. Know that it is highly unlikely nor is it necessary for every faculty member to be enthusiastically involved. Use assessment results as the main argument and gently continue suggesting that common student learning outcomes and assessments be developed across all sections of each general education course.

Use a variety of channels and activities to disseminate course redesign project information

Communication channels might include:

- Project Web page featuring an overview of the project, redesign course descriptions, sample experiential learning and online activities, assessment activities and results, statements of support by administrators, links to course redesign faculty blogs, and links to course redesign resources
- Regular campus-wide forums to demonstrate course redesigns

- Regular institutional publications (See http://NGen.unt.edu/go/BookMaterials for examples)
- Presentations to departments, administrators, student organizations, academic advisors, and any other group that you can persuade to listen
- Course redesign project "collateral" such as pens, bookmarks, and stress balls
- Student recruiting materials that contain Information about the availability of challenging and exciting courses (See http://NGen.unt.edu/go/BookMaterials for examples)
- Course schedules and listings that have designations for redesigned courses (This is particularly important because many redesigned courses do not meet in the usual M-W-F or T-Th format.)

Address the scheduling and space challenges

Most course redesign projects result in courses that have a significantly smaller space footprint especially when multiple sections of the same course redesign are offered. They also often use the scarce large classrooms efficiently. As an example, a two hundred enrollment section of a Principles of Biology class might use the large classroom for one hour once every other week for a large group lecture/testing/housekeeping meeting. This class might require two additional twenty-five seat classrooms three times a week for experiential learning activities. In order to capitalize on the space efficiencies possible in such a course redesign, there needs to be a critical mass of sections of this class or of another course with a similar large classroom usage so that the scarce large classroom resource will be used all three of the meeting slots, e.g., 9–10 a.m. M-W-F. Even if the number and variety of courses exist so that maximum classroom utilization can be achieved, the scheduling and class information systems have to be up to the challenge of making students aware of the non-traditional schedule. Unfortunately, most current classrooms scheduling software is not designed to schedule multiple courses into a single classroom across one time slot.

There needs to be a culture shift away from the "use it or lose it" practice in which classrooms reservations are automatically forwarded to the next term. Faculty need to be encouraged to experiment with classroom utilization without the threat of being sent to the "back of the line" for prime-time classroom assignments.

In addition, providing students with the detailed information regarding the meeting times and locations of their classes is crucial but is also a challenge to most commercial scheduling systems. At the University of North Texas, we decided to design our own course information system that enables tagging of NGen courses and provides the necessary time and location information. See www.UNTeCampus.com.

Of course, as challenging as scheduling classrooms and disseminating accurate information about non-traditional classes is, these tasks are dwarfed by a larger challenge. Colleges and universities are not physically designed to accommodate active and social learning. There needs to be formal flexible space, e.g., classrooms that can be easily altered to accommodate one group of 500 students or twenty groups of 25 students. Space for informal and "semi-formal" learning groups is also very important. As an example, the NGen U.S. History II class includes one ninety-minute class session that includes a mini-lecture for all 200 students and then playing the "What's the Deal" board game in groups of eight. The students leave class and find a place to play the game in designated areas that have been reserved and in any other space where they can set up and play the game.

As new learning spaces are built on campus, it is important that they accommodate flexible and social learning. As an example, the new library at James Madison University has various sized group meeting spaces and all furniture has wheels so that room configurations can change rapidly. Ultimately, we need to be guided by Jefferson's concept of an "academical village," a physical space that promotes shared learning (Hashimshony and Haina, 2006).

Recognize and reward effective teaching

The literature dealing with transforming teaching and learning agrees on two points. First, the tools for designing effective learning are currently available and second, if we are really serious about transforming teaching and learning, we need to find a way to develop a career option that involves sustained attention to teaching and learning without jeopardizing job security, remuneration, or recognition. Of course, recognition of and reward for quality teaching requires the existence of a multifaceted approach to evaluating teaching that is ultimately grounded in the assessment of Student Learning Outcomes.

Changing the reward structure for tenured/tenure-track faculty

If taking part in a significant long-term course redesign project is not to be a career suicide for a tenure track faculty member, one or more of these actions must be considered:

- Revision of the workload policy to include the option of emphasizing teaching
- Recognition of the Scholarship of Teaching and Learning
- Recognition as a publication of courseware that is reviewed and distributed

Developing a career track for instructors

While many general education courses are taught by instructors, such a role is often regarded as temporary until a "real" faculty position becomes available. Creating a path for someone who wants to be involved in innovative teaching in which they can be promoted, earn sabbaticals, and be protected by long-term contracts can encourage the formation of a cadre of course redesign leaders.

Developing a separate administrative unit

While it is important to nurture the teaching role for tenured/tenure-track faculty, such fundamental changes will take time and are vulnerable to changes in administration. The urgency of the need for a fundamental change in how general education courses are delivered may call for creating a separate unit through which redesigned courses can be offered. There is considerable precedence for such units in honors colleges, interdisciplinary colleges, and new colleges. To be most effective, the course redesign unit's administrator will need to have rank equivalent to a dean and report to the chief academic officer. Most likely, the faculty of this unit will be instructors with long-term contracts who are housed together to encourage the development of a Community of Practice. The academic department will be involved in hiring the instructors and will have a role in assuring that the courses taught have equivalent learning outcomes. However, it is important that the instructors report to the administrator of the course redesign unit.

An academic unit dedicated to nurturing and supporting a cadre of faculty with a passion for designing, delivering, assessing, and improving general education courses provides the structure to rapidly develop and deliver enough sections of each course to realize the efficiencies in cost and space made possible by the redesign. More importantly, such an approach can rapidly increase the number of students achieving higher level student learning outcomes.

Conclusion

The history of higher education is littered with the remains of projects to improve teaching and learning. Efforts to change the way in which general education courses are taught need to be long term, carefully planned, have inspired and effective leadership, be understood and supported at all levels of the institution, and sustained by a reward system that recognizes and cultivates quality teaching.

· CHAPTER SIX ·

NEXT GENERATION COURSE REDESIGN IN PRACTICE: FIVE CASES

The NGen course redesign process has resulted in redesigning, teaching, and assessing, a wide variety of large enrollment classes, with a heavy emphasis on general education courses. We are very proud of the NGen Senior Faculty Fellows who have taken the risk and devoted the resources to fundamentally change the learning environment in their course. Choosing the cases to feature in this chapter was very difficult because each NGen course is special and the result of significant effort. The five cases represent a variety of subjects and examples of the NGen model. Each case author was asked to provide information on the following:

- Background of the Redesign
- Synopsis of the Redesigned Course
- Creating the Foundation (SLO's and Assessment Plan)
- The Pedagogy
- Results
- Sustainability and Replication

While the cases contain figures and illustrations, the best way to delve deeper into the work of these NGen Senior Faculty Fellows is to explore the Web materials as indicated throughout the cases.

Dr. Lee Hughes
Assistant Professor, Department of Biological Sciences

Case Study: Redesigning Principles of Biology I

Background of Redesign

Principles of Biology I is the first part of a year-long sequence of introductory biology for biology majors. Previously this course included three hours per week of traditional, minimally-interactive lecture by the course instructor and a one hour "mini-lecture\review" recitation period taught by a graduate teaching assistant. The lecture meetings typically enrolled about 100–200 students each. The recitations, which had originally been added with the intent of providing smaller group help sessions, had grown to around 50 students and no longer functioned as intended. Like many introductory survey courses in the sciences, a high percentage of students, typically 35 to 40 percent, were not successful in the course as taught.

Synopsis of Redesigned Course

The Principles of Biology I course was redesigned into the N-Gen format with the intent to improve student learning and success by combining the best of online and face-to-face instruction. This included designing the course to include more active learning components during face-to-face meetings and to utilize online modules for the majority of content delivery. The combination of in-class meetings and online content is also coordinated to provide repetition of more difficult topics and to allow for self-assessment of learning by the students. Since this is a freshman-level course, the redesign also took into account the need to instill good learning habits in these students and to assist them in transitioning into an unfamiliar course format.

In the redesigned course, students meet each week with the instructor for an hour and a half in a large lecture hall (over 100 students) and in smaller groups (25–30) with a graduate student teaching assistant for an hour-long recitation. Some 40 percent of the course material is delivered through the lecture, with the remaining content given in online course modules. Lectures now include active-learning components and focus more on process and concepts than definitions. The recitations were extensively redesigned and are now devoted to group activities and active learning strategies, while the weekly online lessons provide activities, discussions, external website readings, and homework assignments to reinforce the material.

Assessment is also different in the redesigned course. Previously, 90 percent of the course grade came from lecture exams, with just 10 percent coming from recitation quizzes. In the N-Gen section, multiple types of activities are used to develop the course grade. Lecture exams, which cover about one-third of the course each, now comprises 50 percent of the grade. The assignments and participation portion of the grade is worth 30 percent and consists of online activities, lecture activities, recitation participation, and homework. The remaining 20 percent of the grade comes from lecture and online quizzes. The division of the course grade into these components was developed to emphasize to students the importance of participation in the course activities for their learning. As mentioned previously, a portion of the course philosophy is focused on helping students develop good study habits. For this purpose, the course included numerous weekly activities, all of which contributed to the course grade, to keep the students working with the course content. The course recitations emphasize hands-on activities relating to the course material, while weekly online mastery quizzes help students to assess their familiarity with the content.

Creating the Foundation: Student Learning Outcomes and Assessment

An essential starting point for my redesign of Principles of Biology I was to identify the course objectives. I began by examining the material that was covered in the previous version of the course and used this as a starting point for describing my course objectives. Principles of Biology I is a survey course devoted to exploring cellular biology, genetics, and molecular biology. Upon review of the existing course material I had accumulated in my previous teaching, I was able to identify 13 major content topics that were included in my course. I then set out to state specific learning objectives within each topic. The number of learning objectives per topic area varied from as few as two to as many as nine. It is important to note that each topic does not correspond to a discrete online lesson or lecture meetings, as you will see in the "Pedagogy" section of this case.

The lesson objectives were used as the basis for the construction of a content inventory that would be used as a major component of the overall assessment of the redesigned course. This "introductory biology concept inventory" was specific to the objectives of this course and contained 66 multiple-choice questions, one based on each lesson objective. Care was taken not to focus solely on knowledge recall questions, but to also construct approximately half of the questions at an application or analysis level. The concept inventory was given in a pre-\post-test manner to students in both the traditional and redesigned course sections at the beginning and end of each semester.

The Pedagogy

As noted in the previous section, I did not try to link my course topic areas to the set number of meeting times directly but first defined the topics and learning objectives. My next step was to determine the order and manner in which each of these learning objectives would be incorporated into the course. This might be a somewhat unorthodox approach, since most lesson planning revolves around first defining the individual topics to be covered in each class meeting. However, for my course redesign, I felt that it was important to let the information in the course determine the structure of the course and the mode of delivery.

With the learning objectives defined, I began the process of determining a course schedule and assignment of each objective to a place within either an online lesson or a face-to-face meeting. Based on my previous experiences teaching the course, I was able to make decisions based on the amount of difficulty I could expect students to experience with different types of material. This helped me to determine the amount of exposure students needed to a content topic. With material that was fundamentally easier for students to understand, such as the chemical building blocks of life, little repetition in coverage was necessary. These topics were placed in the schedule such that they were covered directly only once or twice in the overall course plan, typically once in either a face-to-face or online lecture with some reinforcement during recitation. For more difficult topics, additional repetition was built into the schedule. A complex topic such as glucose metabolism would be covered in multiple ways, including online and face-to-face lessons along with recitation activities.

The type of information also helped to determined the delivery format, as did the time demands of a weekly course. As I looked at the course schedule and learning objective list, many objectives in the course fell into a logical sequential order of presentation. Structurally in the course, this meant that if a particular set of objectives were presented in one lesson (either online or face-to-face), then the next set would have to be delivered in the other format since lessons of necessity must alternate in delivery method due to the course structure. Thus, each decision I made about a lesson had to take into account the topics immediately before and after that lesson and the manner in which they would be presented. As I worked out these details, I began to see this process of moving between delivery formats and recitation activities as somewhat akin to a dance, in this case much like a waltz back and forth across the ballroom of introductory biology.

Lecture

From a basic standpoint, the 80 minute lecture period once per week is still quite similar in format to a traditional lecture course, with the majority of class led by an instructor in a large lecture hall. However, it is fundamentally different in several ways. First of all, because the lecture meeting is preceded by an online lesson and required activities, including the mastery quiz, there is a higher degree of expectation that students will arrive to class prepared to move on to the next lesson objectives. Second, less total lecture time is spent on delivery of new content. These two factors allow more focus in lecture on exploring processes and tying together concepts, rather than simply trying to cover content as is common in survey courses of this type. Overall, the format of the lecture is flexible enough to allow a portion of class time to be spent on active learning strategies such as discussions, demonstrations, or group problem solving. As an example, when I taught the course in a traditional format, I would spend most of a lecture period discussing eukaryotic cell structure and function. Because I had to introduce and cover the topic within that one lecture, I typically spent most of the lesson describing the parts of the cell and their basic function, but only had a few minutes at the end to dicuss how these parts worked as a whole. Now, with the blended format class, students receive the basic cell structure and function information online. When they arrive for the weekly lecture, I can spend time integrating this information. I begin by having them complete a group exercise to compare and contrast the features of prokaryotic and eukaryotic cells. I then show them how various cell organelles can work together by following the synthesis and transport of a secretory protein. I end the lesson by exploring endosymbiotic theory with the class. This is a much more indepth coverage of the complex issues in this topic than in the previous format.

Online

Each week of the course contains one online module that becomes available immediately following the lecture meeting and which is due immediately

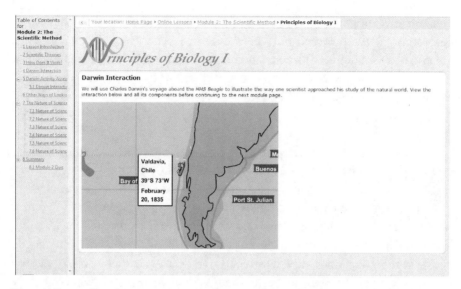

Figure 1 Darwin Interactive

preceding the next. Each module consists of a number of web pages that deliver new content. There is at least one graded activity in each module that helps to reinforce the new material, such as a discussion or assignment. Modules may also contain a number of non-graded activities such as a Flash interactive or an external website to help them explore the topic. Upon completing the contents of each module, students then take a graded mastery quiz. This quiz, which consists of a subset of questions from a small question bank, may be taken multiple times during the week-long period that the module is available. Student are given the highest grade from their attempts. However, to insure that they have a strong grasp of the module's information, they must make at least a grade of 70 percent in order to receive credit on that week's quiz. See Figures 1 and 2 for screen shots of Darwin and nucleotide interactives.

The full Web interactive for the nucleotide exercise can be found at http:\\NGen.unt.edu\go\BookMaterials

Recitation

The hour long recitation period each week provides an opportunity to reinforce the concepts that the students have learned in both the lecture and online components of the course. These recitation sections are smaller, with only 25–30 students each, which allows more interaction among all the section members. Each recitation consists of a hands-on activity that involves a

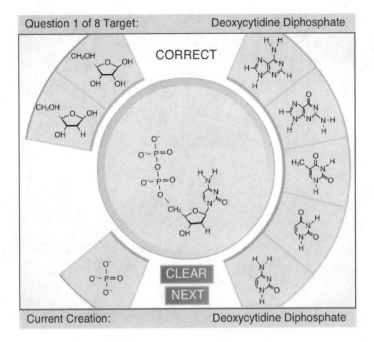

Figure 2 Nucleotide Interactive

recent course topic. This might be an activity in a small group or pair, or could be an activity involving the entire class. Examples of these activities include recitation meetings where teams of students compete in a "Jeopardy"-like game show, a whole-class activity where the students act out the process of mitosis, and several case studies. See Figure 3 for photo of students playing the "Parts of a Cell Beauty Contest."

Results

Several methods were employed in the N-Gen Principles of Biology I course to assess student learning and measure student satisfaction with the redesigned course. This included the concept inventory pre-\post-test, a comparison of student success in the course, a student assessment of learning gains, and surveys.

Concept inventory

Data were collected for students in both the traditional and blended sections of the course during the Fall 2007, Spring 2008, and Fall 2008 semesters.

Figure 3 "Parts of a Cell Beauty Contest"

Comparison data was available on 248 students from the blended course and 155 from the traditional format course. No differences were noted between the blended and traditional samples for pre-test inventory scores, final letter grade distribution, and ethnic or gender composition. There was a significant difference for the mean of change between pre- and post-test. The average gain for blended students was 12.3, while that of traditional students was 8.9.

Student success

Following the pilot semester of the redesigned course, the trend for student success (those students making an A, B, or C) in the N-Gen course has been higher than that of students in the traditional sections. The N-Gen section success rates have been 60.2% for Fall 2006, 66% for Spring 2007, 73.3% for Fall 2007, 69.9% for Spring 2008, and 72.7% for Fall 2008. For the same time period, traditional section success rates were 67%, 61%, 57.7%, 55.1%, and 64.9% respectively.

Student Assessment of Learning Gains

The Student Assessment of Learning Gains (SALG) was created for Principles of Biology I at the SALG Website (http:\\www.salgsite.org\). Only students who had experienced the blended course completed this instrument, in which they were asked to rank course components from not helpful (1) to very much help (5). Student rankings for the class lecture, recitation, and online components were all positive (average ranking of 3 or above). Students found the online course modules to be the most helpful course component, with almost 84% giving a rank of 4 or 5. The weekly online quizzes also ranked highly, with 78% giving a 4 or 5. On the other hand, some students had a more negative reaction to some course components. While still having an average ranking of more than 3, the recitations and the recitation group activities received rankings of 1 or 2 from almost 25% of the students.

Surveys

Students in the course were given an attitude toward biology survey and an N-Gen survey. The attitude of the students in the both versions of the course was measured at the beginning and end of the course. While the mean change was negative in both groups, the change for students in the blended section was less negative, though not significantly so. The other survey was given to blended section students at the end of the course. They were asked the following question: "If you were to start this course over again, would you prefer a traditional face-to-face format, or would you prefer the N-Gen (blended) redesign format you are experiencing?" The students' responses were overwhelmingly positive, with 80% indicating that they would choose the blended version again.

Sustainability and Replication

After all the work put into redesigning Principles of Biology I, my long term goal is that the N-Gen version of the course continue to be taught and that it be expanded to additional sections. As part of the process of redesign, I have tried to develop instructor notes and information to assist others who may teach sections using my course materials.

From a standpoint of sustainability, the N-Gen version does not require significant resources as compared to the traditional section. After the initial investment of developing the materials for the course, the actual teaching of the course requires about the same amount of departmental resources. The only additional resource utilized in this case relates to the graduate teaching assistant for the recitation. In the traditional course sections, teaching assistants are responsible for sections containing 50–60 students, while the blended sections have only 25–30 students each. Thus, it does work out to a higher total number of recitation sections that must be provided for and covered by graduate students compared with the traditional format.

The N-Gen Process

Developing, implementing, and teaching an N-Gen course is a large, but fulfilling task. From the very beginning of the process, I found the process to be an especially liberating exercise as an instructor. We rarely have an opportunity to stop what we are doing and really examine the creative options that we might apply to our teaching. After experiencing this process, I think that it is an important thing to do. Often, we forge ahead with what is familiar, when both ourselves and our students might benefit from a fresh look at the entire course, including the material to be covered, our expectations for the students, and how we help the students meet those expectations. The redesign process allowed me to be creative in how I did these things, which was a very satisfying exercise.

One important component of the N-Gen process was the community of practice. By involving faculty in small groups during the redesign, there was a sense of common purpose and synergy that helps everyone involved. It was helpful to have a peer group with whom to share the process. This ranged from having someone to share your exciting ideas with to having a group with whom to commiserate when things weren't going smoothly. There was also a vertical component in our community of practice. Not only were we able to share with our peer group of redesigners, but we also had access to those faculty who had gone through the process before us. We in turn could offer our advice to those groups who came later.

The community of practice was not only a support network but it was also an amazing source of creative ideas. Although we each come from different disciplines and teach courses that are quite different in content type, we found common elements in our redesigns as well as adaptable ideas. As one example, while watching an animation created for a history instructor that showed the exchange of goods and diseases between the new and old worlds, I came up with an idea for an animation that features Charles Darwin's voyage aboard the *H.M.S. Beagle* (see Figure 1). I know there were other examples of this type of synergy between faculty who were part of this community of practice.

Overall, I have enjoyed being part of the N-Gen process and think that it has been both a positive process from a professional standpoint and has shown to be an improved approach in terms of student learning outcomes. It is also an ongoing process, as I continue to tweak my approaches to the course delivery, content, and activities.

Dr. Robert G. Insley
Associate Professor, Department of Management

Case Study: Redesigning Communicating in Business

Background of redesign

Communicating in Business is a one-semester core course in the College of Business. Most of the students are junior-level business majors who are required to take the course. The annual enrollment is approximately 1,380 students taught in multiple sections by many different instructors, with class sizes ranging from 30–240 students. The redesigned sections include predominately large-enrollment classes, along with a few mid-size and small-enrollment sections. Prior to course redesign, the dominant instructional approach in the face-to-face sections was lecturing and testing. The lecture\test approach contributed to the following problems: compromised student learning, an overall lowering of course grades leading to more failures, high numbers of withdrawals and drops, high absence rates, minimal class discussion, little interaction among students in and outside of class, and little student interaction with the course material beyond memorizing information for tests. Each of these problems represented missed opportunities to better serve the students.

Synopsis of redesigned course

In the redesigned N-Gen Communicating in Business class, students are introduced to course content via a number of sources that include lectures, assigned readings, class speakers, in-class exercises, team activities, and online activities. The redesign efforts moved the instructional approach from purely lecture-based to one in which students are more engaged with the course content, fellow students, and their instructor.

The central goals that drove the redesign effort focused on reducing the number and length of lectures and getting students more engaged with the course content, fellow students, and their instructor. Engagement was meant to increase student success rates, while simultaneously reducing failure, withdrawal, and drop rates. Another redesign goal was to integrate problem solving and higher levels of critical thinking into the course as a means of improving student understanding, retention, and success. Additionally, an outcomes-based assessment plan was needed to determine the extent to which the above goals were being met and to provide feedback necessary to drive necessary revisions.

With the above goals in mind, my redesign efforts were focused on developing clear learning outcomes to which all course instruction, student requirements, and assessment were linked. Then I set out to determine a variety of instructional approaches that would get the students more engaged and also provide them with numerous hands-on experiential activities so that they would be "doing" much of the course content, as opposed to merely memorizing it.

Students in the N-Gen sections of Communicating in Business meet face-to-face in class approximately 47 percent of the time allocated to the course. While the face-to-face class sessions involve some lecture, there are also numerous in-class team exercises. Some of the face-to-face class time is set aside for students to work with fellow teammates on an extensive team project.

The remaining 53 percent of the time allocated to the course is set aside for students to come together outside of class to complete the team project and online activities. The team project is designed to give the students hands-on exposure to a number of the course topics, as well as increasing interaction with their classmates. The online activities include a syllabus quiz, chapter quizzes, and a variety of course content-based exercises ranging in format from cases and drop-and-drag exercises to gaming and video exercises. The online activities are designed to increase course content understanding and retention. Course grades are based on two exams, in-class activities, online activities, and the team project.

Creating the foundation: Student learning outcomes and assessment

The redesign process leading to the N-Gen Business Communication course configuration began with the development of an outcomes-based assessment plan. The plan was designed to coordinate instruction, grade components, and performance assessment with major course goals and student learning outcomes in order to ensure that necessary materials are addressed and assessed. The steps included defining the major course goals, student learning outcomes, learning strategies, and assessment strategies. Each step is described below.

The first step involved determining the major course goals that meet college, university, and state standards and expectations for the core business communication course. Examples include making the students effective listeners and business writers and speakers.

Once the major course goals were determined, I wrote the student learning outcomes. The result was twenty-three learning outcomes that include the following examples: (A) Upon completion of the course, students will be able to describe communication techniques that impede and contribute to effective business meetings. (B) Upon completion of the course, students will be able to identify and demonstrate the various skills necessary to give an effective business presentation.

After the student learning outcomes were written, I determined the specific learning strategies necessary to achieve each of the twenty-three student learning outcomes. The following two examples are the learning strategies for the two student learning outcomes presented above. (A) Repetition and reinforcement throughout the course using class discussion, online and in-class quizzes and exercises, instructional video exercises, interaction during team meetings, and reading assignments. (B) Repetition and reinforcement throughout the course using class discussion, online and in-class quizzes and exercises, reading assignments, and a videotaped team presentation.

Once the learning strategies were finalized, I determined assessment strategies for each of the student learning outcomes. The following two examples are the assessment strategies for the two student learning outcomes presented above. (A) Pre- and post-tests, online quizzes, in-class exercises such as the Interpersonal Skills Inventory self assessment instrument, critical analysis of instructional videos, and exams. (B) Pre- and post-tests, online quizzes, in-class exercises such as How Good Are Your Presentation Skills self-assessment exercise, critical analysis of instructional videos and in-class team presentations, and exams.

In summary, the plan was designed to align instruction, grade components, and assessment instruments with major course goals and student learning outcomes to ensure that necessary materials are addressed and assessed.

The Pedagogy

Communicating in Business is a survey course that addresses a variety of topics ranging from teaming and business writing to intercultural communication and business presentations. The amount of time devoted to each topic and the related activities vary based on what is needed to adequately address each.

In turn, there are common instructional approaches crossing all topics including pre-tests and post-tests, textbook readings, lectures and in-class exercises, the team project, online activities, and exams. These are described below. With the exception of the assigned textbook readings, the other instructional approaches are designed to get the students more engaged with the course content (e.g., online activities & team project) and\or interacting more with fellow students (e.g., team project & in-class team exercises).

Pre-Tests and Post-Tests

I administer two pre-tests and two post-tests each semester. Pre-test 1 is administered during the first or second class session and is followed up mid-way through the semester with post-test 1. Pre-test 2 is administered during the first class session following post-test 1 and is followed up at the end of the semester with post-test 2 which is the final exam. Each pre-test helps me determine the students' level of familiarization with the subject matter I will cover during the related period. The post-tests, in turn, help me assess degrees of learning and need for revision.

Textbook readings

Each course topic is supported by one or more textbook chapters. The students are encouraged to read each chapter or set of chapters related to a single topic before the topic is addressed in class and before doing the related online activities. The general thought regarding these expectations is that the students will get more out of the classes and online activities by doing so.

Lectures and in-class exercises

Lectures are fewer and shorter in length and are limited to addressing important material that needs to be stressed, material that is typically difficult for students to understand, and material that is controversial and invites discussion. Lectures are as much question-and-answer sessions as traditional lectures. For example, instead of just putting up Power Point slides containing bulleted lists for them to copy into their notes, I will often share the desired information through questions either presented via Power Point or verbal promptings.

Face-to-face class sessions are not just about lectures. Instead, they are either a mixture of lecture and in-class activities or exclusively hands-on, in-class activities. Students are assigned to a seating chart based on team formation to facilitate in-class team exercises and team project meetings and to increase the amount of communication among team project members before class starts, during class breaks, and at the end of class. In-class exercises are typically cases, discussion questions, and instructional video exercises.

Team project

The team project is a critical component of the course in that it not only gets the students interacting with fellow students but it also actively engages the students with approximately 85 percent of the course subject matter. The project requires critical thinking on the part of the students, uses a number of creative pedagogical techniques that engage students in the learning process, and incorporates the use of new and emerging technologies.

Each team assumes the role of a consulting group that was hired to either bring a company up to speed on how to use a given type of business communication technology or on how to communicate effectively in business settings with business people from another country. Students are required to conduct necessary research with the guidance and assistance of one of our business librarians who has set up special online research sites for our team project. The business librarian visits with the students in class at the start of the project to launch the research component. Once the teams have completed the research phase, they are required to write a formal business report that is followed up with a team presentation. This project assists in preparing the students for their business careers, as well as for similar requirements in the capstone policy class they are required to take the last semester of their senior year.

Each team is required to have a team leader or, if they wish, co-leaders. A variety of forms are collected from teams and individual team members as they move through the project. Forms such as the *Team Leader and Individual Task Assignments Form* and the *Research Summary Form* are intended to keep students on a realistic schedule. See http:\\NGen.unt.edu\go\BookMaterials for samples of these two forms. Forms such as the *Team Leader Progress Form, Team Project Evaluation Form—Research & Report Phases, Team Project Evaluation Form—Presentation Phase* are included to determine an individuals' level of involvement and interaction. A sample of the Team Leader Progress Form can be found at http:\\NGen.unt.edu\go\BookMaterials. In addition, teams are required to submit a draft copy of the report so I can provide them with some pre-editing phase feedback and so they have sufficient time to edit their report before the final version is due. Also there is an online discussion site for each team that provides one more medium to facilitate frequent communication and to support team efforts. Students are also encouraged to use online teaming tools and software and online collaborative writing tools to support their efforts.

Online activities

The online activities represent yet another way the students are actively engaged with the course content. These activities are designed to reinforce learning and help students identify subject matter they either do not understand or are not sufficiently familiar with so they can learn more and perform better on exams and the team project. The online activities include a syllabus quiz that reminds students about key course policies, chapter quizzes, and exercises that range in format from drop-and-drag and gaming formats to cases and video exercises. Each online exercise is followed-up with a quiz to test comprehension and retention.

Exams

Two exams are administered. One is the mid-term exam and the other the final exam. These are actually post-tests 1 & 2 or some variation of each. The assigned textbook readings, lectures, in-class activities, and team project are all designed, in part, to help students achieve higher success rates on the course exams. The exams help me assess degrees of learning.

In summary, students are assessed and assigned points on in-class exercises, the team project, online activities, and exams. The grade weighting is as follows: in-class exercises – 10%, team project – 25% (report – 10%, presentation – 5%, and individual involvement & interaction – 10%), online activities – 25%, and exams – 40% (Exam 1 – 20% & Exam 2 – 20%).

Results

The following results are based on the time period ranging from Fall semester 2007 through Spring semester 2009 during which time the redesigned Communicating in Business course has been up and running. Here I will report on evidence of student support for the innovation, the innovation's enhancement of teaching effectiveness, the innovation's contribution to achieving course objectives, and peer recognition of the innovation.

Evidence of student support for the innovation

One source of evidence comes from the *Preference for Course Format: N-Gen or FTF Survey*, which I administer online during the last two weeks of each term.

Larger percentages of both successful students (students who earned an A, B, or C) and unsuccessful students (students who earned a D, F, or withdrew from the course) have reported preference for the N-Gen format in contrast with the traditional face-to-face (FTF) format, with higher percentages of successful students preferring the N-Gen format than unsuccessful students. For example, when we look at Fall 2008 classes that followed the N-Gen format, 16 percent more favored the N-Gen format (58 percent vs. 42%).

A second source of evidence comes from the 21-item *Survey of Student Attitude Toward Subject of Course* that I administer online during the second and last week of each semester. For example, during Spring 2008 seven of the thirteen positive statements on the survey showed increases in the N-Gen sections when contrasted with the Fall 2007 N-Gen sections. And of the eight negative statements on the survey, seven showed a decrease in the Spring 2008 N-Gen sections when contrasted with the Fall 2007 N-Gen sections. Examples of positive statements that show statistically significant difference (sig. .05) follow: (+.31) *I like this subject.* (+.39) *I know a lot about this subject.* and (+.33) *This subject is easy to learn.*

Evidence that the innovation enhances teaching effectiveness

Records show that student success rates have increased and student failure rates have decreased since we switched to the N-Gen format. Student success refers to students earning letter grades of A, B, & C. Student failure refers to students earning letter grades of either D or F and to those who withdrew from or dropped the course. Looking back at the Fall 2005 through Spring 2007 sections taught using the traditional face-to-face (FTF) format, 79 percent of the students succeeded and 21 percent failed. When we looked at the Fall 2007 through Fall 2008 sections taught using the N-Gen format, we found that 84 percent of the students succeeded and 16 percent failed. The N-Gen format resulted in a five percent increase in the number of students who succeeded in the course.

Furthermore, when we looked just at the changes across the Fall 2007 through Fall 2008 N-Gen sections, we noted steady upward growth in success rates and steady decline in failure rates. In Fall 2007, 82 percent succeeded and 18 percent failed. In Spring 2008, 83 percent succeeded and 17 percent failed. In Fall 2008, 87 percent succeeded and 13 percent failed.

I believe that higher student success rates in N-Gen sections are clearly related to the development of clear learning outcomes that link course content, activities, and performance assessment as well as the blended instructional format that more actively engages the students.

Evidence of peer recognition for the innovation

I am a Quality Enhancement Plan (QEP) Senior Faculty Fellow, the QEP representative for the College of Business, a Level 1 Assessment Facilitator through the University's Center for Learning, Assessment, and Redesign, and a member of the University's steering committee, which is exploring the feasibility of expanding the Community of Practitioners concept outside of the N-Gen Project across campus. I have made presentations regarding different redesign aspects and assessment outcomes at the following conferences: the Southwestern Educational Research Association Conference, the Texas Association for Institutional Research Association, the Facilitating Significant Learning Conference, and the Transforming Large Enrollment Classes Symposium. I have also given presentations about my redesign efforts and outcomes at two QEP\N-Gen Retreats, one QEP\N-Gen Forum, and one department workshop.

Sustainability and replication

As for sustainability, I don't foresee a threat to the N-Gen approach to our Communicating in Business course short of the infusion of a new set of instructors and administrators who have both the desire and power to move the course in a different direction. I don't see any evidence of this from our current faculty and administrators. In fact, the N-Gen approach is consistent with a growing national trend toward performance assessment and using instructional approaches that engage students with the course content and fellow students, which appears to be an approach better received by Millennial students than the traditional lecture approach. N-Gen courses are well received at our university and the number of N-Gen courses and blended-course variations being offered is growing. Since its inception, the N-Gen Communicating in Business course has expanded from large-enrollment sections into both mid-size and small sections smoothly.

I believe the N-Gen Communicating in Business course could be easily replicated given the structure that is currently in place, a structure that links together major course goals, student learning outcomes, learning strategies, and assessment strategies. As long as others adhere to the course structure, they can replicate this course. This doesn't suggest that others would need to use the same textbook, although they would need to use one that includes the same topics. Furthermore, they could work in other online and in-class activities as they saw fit as long as they adhered to the structural plan.

Each time I consider making a revision, which I am constantly doing, I first make sure it is grounded in the structural plan. This was the case when at the end of Spring 2008 I realized that not setting interim deadlines for team project components impeded teams' ability to meet major project deadlines, perform at desired quality levels, and work together cohesively. In response, starting Fall 2008 I started the team project approximately two weeks earlier and added interim activities, forms, and due dates to alleviate the above concerns. For example, I added a Research Summary Form and due date that moved the research phase along at a reasonable pace, so teams would be able to start writing the report at a reasonable point in time and not be upset with fellow teammates who were dragging their heels meeting their research requirements. I also added a pre-edited report requirement and built in a due date for it to provide teams with some degree of feedback and assure adequate time for them to edit their reports before the final due date. Such changes have been well received by the students and have contributed to improved performance. I believe this is the case because the students recognize the changes help them perform better, help them get along with fellow teammates better, and help them meet deadlines.

As time and funds allow, I hope to write and produce additional interactive instructional videos for the course on topics such as business presentations, job interviews, listening, and customer service communication, like the business meetings video I have already created. Additionally, I plan to test the practicality and benefits of using the online grading and digital mark-up tool *GradeMark* to evaluate the team project reports. I also plan to help a greater number of student teams become actively involved in using wikis as an additional tool for their team project and assist them in using the collaborative writing tool on the university's new online EagleConnect system. I plan to broaden the number of topics addressed in the team project, as well as add more in-class activities as a means of further engaging the students with the course material and fellow students.

The N-Gen process

The N-Gen process is an outgrowth of the university's Quality Enhancement Plan (QEP), which was developed as part of the reaccreditation requirements for SACS. A central feature of the N-Gen program is the Community of Practice (CoP), which is an interdisciplinary community of instructors who come together each month for brown bag seminars and meetings to share ideas and methodologies. It is genuinely exciting to learn about creative approaches firsthand and to then reflect on whether these approaches or variations of them will work effectively in the Communicating in Business course. In addition, CoP members brainstorm solutions for instructional approaches that are not working smoothly. The fact that CoP members come together from a vast range of disciplines makes each of us think outside of the box and our comfort zones, which often results in creative and useful solutions we wouldn't have arrived at on our own. This approach of bringing together faculty from several disciplines for obvious practical reasons has received enough positive recognition to date that our university has formed a steering committee that is exploring the feasibility of expanding the Community of Practice concept outside of the N-Gen Project across campus.

The N-Gen process, however, is not without its challenges. While instructional and performance assessment expectations of students, administrators, and legislators are changing, it is difficult for some faculty to adjust accordingly. Major redesign efforts like those the N-Gen process require are time consuming and require instructors to move away from some or most of the course structure and instructional approaches with which they are most comfortable. Once the course is redesigned, there is also the ongoing challenge to break away from prior instructional approaches that have often defined their teaching styles. Furthermore, instructors who embrace the N-Gen process are challenged to make time to be active members of the Community of Practice, to analyze assessment feedback, and to make necessary revisions based on assessment feedback and CoP input.

There are several ways these challenges can be addressed. For example, a strong Community of Practice can motivate and guide instructors through the redesign phase and beyond. Supportive deans, department chairs, and colleagues who understand and appreciate the goals of the N-Gen redesign can also be motivational. Furthermore, department, college, and\or university support in the way of necessary resources is critical. For example, providing release time (reduced workload) during the redesign phase is encouraged. Other examples include funding for other resources such as the purchase of films, video cameras, etc. In addition, funding support for teaching assistants is encouraged, especially with large-enrollment classes.

No matter our personal thoughts and preferences as faculty and administrators, the changes addressed in the N-Gen redesign process embrace a reality that cannot be ignored. In response, universities and colleges are challenged to create courses in which students are more actively engaged with both the subject matter and fellow students, problem solving and critical thinking are emphasized, and performance assessment is directly linked to learning outcomes, and is analyzed to provide feedback needed to spearhead necessary revisions.

Dr. Kelly Donahue-Wallace
Associate Professor and Division Chair, Art Education and History

Dr. Denise Baxter
Assistant Professor, Art Education and History

Case Study: Redesigning Art History Survey II

Background of redesign

Art History Survey II engages with the art and architecture of Europe, the United States, and selected non-Western cultures from 1400 to the present and is offered once annually in a single section of approximately 300 students. It is a required course for all majors in the College of Visual Arts and Design and fulfils university core curriculum requirements. It has been taught by both ladder-rank and adjunct faculty in a lecture-based format of three, fifty minutes lectures per week over the course of the semester, with three Teaching Assistants doing much of the grading. While lectures stressed concepts, assessments, typically 3–4 exams and 2–3 papers, emphasized recall over critical thinking. As a result, students arrived in upper-level courses without the content knowledge or critical thinking skills necessary to succeed and without a good sense of the discipline of art history.

Synopsis of redesigned course

The NGen Art History Survey II focuses on developing skills that are grounded in the methodological approaches of the discipline of art history. Rather than a machine-gun approach by which students might encounter as many works as possible per lecture hour, the revised course is divided into seven, two-week modules. Each module focuses on a primary example of a period style approached through a defined methodological approach. For example, the Renaissance period style is exemplified through Raphael's painting of the *School of Athens* (1509–11). This painting serves as the fulcrum around which the lecture is constructed using other works of art and architecture to define the period style. It additionally models two modes of analysis: formal and iconographic. The redesigned class consequently presents fewer works of art and architecture but each one to a greater depth. Rather than employ commercially-available textbooks, known for their superficial treatment and authoritative voice, instead students read online content authored by the instructors, scholarly essays and articles, primary documents, art criticism, and other types of readings. What the course lacks in breadth—skipping over several artistic movements since the Renaissance—it therefore supplements with depth.

The content redesign is accompanied by structural changes. The class meets as a whole for one lecture per week on Mondays in which the primary object for the module is contextualized in various manners and the goals for each module are established. The remainder of the weeks (Wednesdays and Fridays) is given over to small group, break-out sessions with discussion and problem-solving activities led by the instructor and three Teaching Assistants. The meeting days for the groups rotate as do the instructor or TA with whom they meet, giving students the opportunity to work closely with the entire instructional team, including the professor. See Figure 4 for the organization of each two-week module.

The small group sessions present active learning opportunities. Students prepare for these by reading the online course content and scholarly texts and answering reading questions in advance of the group meetings. The sessions offer the opportunity to discuss the readings and to raise questions. Students interact directly with peers and instructors in conversations privileging higher order thinking. They additionally practice the types of activities required for each module's major assessment (described below) and receive grades for the quality and quantity of their participation.

The third essential facet of the redesign is the introduction of Problem-Based Learning (PBL). Time outside of class is used to solve each module's Problem-Based Learning-style challenge. There are seven challenges in the course and each presents students with "real life" scenarios, reflecting the real work of the discipline of art history. The challenges are focused on objects and monuments from local public and museum collections, allowing students to deal with objects and monuments on a first-hand basis. The methodology of each is keyed to the approach modeled in lecture in the unit. In the first module, for example, students act as research assistants for the university, classifying the form and iconography of works of Renaissance art from a fictitious donation to the university. In another module, students construct a walking tour of a nearby college, analyzing the site's rhetorical program after studying a similar program at Versailles. A third PBL assignment has a contemporary artist known for her aggressive treatment of racial issues redesigning a local Civil War memorial. Students imagine her solution and justification of the design, then switch hats and argue against the new monument from the perspective of a local shop owner. Rather than memorization of content, the course focuses on application of content and the exercise of skills.

Weekly Schedule

	Monday (everyone comes to class)	Wednesday (only the 4 groups listed below come to class on Wednesdays of the week listed)				Friday (only the 4 groups listed below come to class on Wednesdays of the week listed)			
Week 1	Lecture (Module begins)	Group A Room 1 Instructor	Group B Room 2 TA 1	Group C Room 3 TA 2	Group D Room 4 TA 3	Group E Room 1 Instructor	Group F Room 2 TA 1	Group G Room 3 TA 2	Group H Room 4 TA 3
Week 2	Lecture (Module continues)	Group I Room 1 Instructor	Group J Room 2 TA 1	Group K Room 3 TA 2	Group L Room 4 TA 3	Group M Room 1 Instructor	Group N Room 2 TA 1	Group O Room 3 TA 2	Group P Room 4 TA 3

Figure 4 Two-Week Module Schedule

The decision to revise the course in this direction came after discussion among the art history faculty as a whole about the possible benefits to our students of a modified PBL model. Applications of PBL in the humanities in general, and in art history in particular, are somewhat unusual and are typically limited to courses with small enrollments.[1] However, the real-world scenarios adapted from this model for a large-enrollment course allow for the practical application of concepts and reintegration of factual knowledge, thereby facilitating the departmentally-based goals that the NGen course prepare students for upper-division course work in art history by better representing art history as a discipline within lower level courses and by increasing higher-order thinking in lower level courses. More significantly, it is our hope that the revised model will help to improve the critical thinking skills of our students, thereby assisting them in their course of university study – whatever it may be – but also preparing them to engage in rational, critical debate within the public sphere. The PBL activities additionally allow the instructors to make greater use of the rich resources of the greater Dallas-Fort Worth area: museums, universities, and even shopping malls, which are analyzed in one PBL activity for their constructions of gender and class.

Creating the foundation: Student learning outcomes and assessment

The redesign process was the impetus for a reconsideration and redefinition of the desired learning outcomes for the course and how these might be best

---

[1] See, for instance, Molly Lindler, "Problem-Based Learning in the Art-History Survey Course," *CAA News* 30, no. 5 (September 2005).

assessed. In so doing it became evident that the iterated course goals were neither being adequately assessed by the extant course, nor were they in keeping with the actual faculty-desired outcomes for the course. Because Art History Survey II fulfils university core requirements, is a required course for all students in the College of Visual Arts and Design (current enrolment is more than 2000), and is one of the cornerstones for the Art History major, it was necessary to consider three interrelated tiers of student learning outcomes: Institutional, Departmental, and Course.

Institutional

The Institutional tier includes those requirements stipulated within Visual and Performing Arts core component area.[2] These are broad in scope as befits the fact that a divergent range of courses are intended to meet their terms. As per these Institutional objectives, throughout a successful completion of Art History Survey II a student will:

1. Demonstrate awareness of the scope and variety of works of art.
2. Understand those works as expressions of individual and human values within an historical and social context.
3. Demonstrate knowledge of the influence of literature, philosophy, and\or the arts on intercultural experiences.
4. Develop an appreciation for the aesthetic principles that guide or govern the artistic production within discrete periods and eras.

---

[2] The Univeristy of North Texas Core has undergone revision and the new Core Curriculum will go into effect in the 2010–2011 academic year. Art History Survey II is slated to continue to fulfil the redefined Visual and Performing Arts core component area, whose sanctioned Exemplary Educational Objectives include:

To demonstrate awareness of the scope and variety of works in the arts.

1. To understand those works as expressions of individual and human values within diverse historical, social and cultural contexts.
2. To engage in a creative process or interpretive act in order to comprehend the physical and intellectual demands required of the author or visual\ performing artist.
3. To develop an appreciation for the aesthetic principles that guide or govern the arts.

Departmental

The course is additionally assessed for department learning objectives, the results of which are supplied to accrediting agencies. Rather than functioning as a strategic benchmark for accomplishing the university's core exemplary learning objectives,[3] the departmental goals are those objectives of the internal assessment strategy of the Art History area within the Department of Art Education and Art History that this course is intended to facilitate. Student success or failure in meeting these objectives would then be reported to external accrediting agencies such as the National Association of Schools of Art and Design (college-level accreditation for the College of Visual Arts and Design) or the Southern Association of Colleges and Schools (university-level accreditation for the University of North Texas as a whole). While there is clearly a relationship between the Institutional and Departmental goals, one does not function as a subset of the other. The Departmental goals that Art History Survey II is intended to assess include student ability to do the following:

1. Employ the specialized vocabulary of the discipline of art history.
2. Identify key objects and monuments within a breadth of discrete periods and regions of artistic production.
3. Demonstrate knowledge of the history and literature of methodologies employed in art history.

Student achievement of the departmental learning objectives are assessed in an entry assessment completed by new art history majors as they finish Art History Survey II.

Course

Course goals, therefore, follow upon both University and Departmental goals, offering more specific explications of both, but also delineating objectives felt by the Art History faculty to be necessary for successful completion of an

---

[3] See Dr. Tracey M. Gau's World Literature case study in this volume for an example of university, departmental, and course goals that work in the manner of a strategic plan in this regard.

Art History Survey II course. According to these objectives, upon successful completion of the course a student will be able to:

1. Perform formal, iconographic, and functional analyses of objects and monuments within their social and historical contexts.
2. Demonstrate knowledge of several methodologies employed by art historians.
3. Apply the appropriate method to the discussion of an object or monument.
4. Employ the vocabulary specific to the visual arts and the discipline of art history.
5. Identify an array of objects and monuments created between 1300 and the present.
6. Compare the general formal, iconographic, and functional characteristics of the major artistic period styles from 1400-the present.
7. Analyze the function and intention of art exhibitions.

Module

These three-tiered course goals are then expressed to the student on a module-by-module basis in lesson outcomes statements that commence the online component of each of the seven two-week modules, and in the grading rubrics used to assess each module's performative (in-class discussion and problem-solving exercises in small groups) and constructed responses (the student solutions to the PBL-based challenges).[4] In the first course module, for example, which focuses on Raphael's *School of Athens* and formal and iconographic methodologies and requires students to analyze the fictitious donation of Renaissance art, students are presented with the following set of lesson outcomes informing them that by the end of the module they should be able to do the following:

1. Analyze the formal characteristics of a work of art that employs Renaissance pictorial principles. (Course Objectives 1, 2, and 3)
2. Analyze the iconographic characteristics of a work of art that employs narrative. (Course Objectives 1, 2 and 3)

---

[4] Please note that while the desired outcomes are listed at the start of each module, the relationship between these and Institutional, Departmental, and Course Objectives are not. Rather than instructive, this level of transparency would be cumbersome for the student. The same is true of the annotations on the grading rubric below.

3. Employ the terminology and concepts relevant to the art and architecture of the Italian Renaissance period. (Departmental Objective 1, Course Objective 4)
4. Identify and compare a related object or monuments (Institutional Objectives 1 and 4; Departmental Objective 2; Course Objectives 5 and 6)

These outcomes can then be clearly matched to the grading rubrics for each module. Again, let us take the first module as an example. The challenge with which students are presented is to provide a formal and iconographic analysis of an unknown narrative painting that demonstrates characteristics of Italian Renaissance period style. The elements of the rubric concerning light, color, space, and composition relate to formal analysis, the others concern iconography, and all assess the employment of terminology and concepts relevant to Renaissance period style (See Figure 5.)

In this manner, the relationship between overarching course and lesson objectives is linked for the student to the ways they will actually be graded—the assignment rubrics. At the same time, for purposes of both departmental and institutional assessment, the individual elements of these rubrics can be tracked through Course, Departmental, and Institutional objectives.

GRADING RUBRIC

Here is the rubric we will employ to grade your work.

Student...	Assessment of characteristics				
	1 Poor	2	3 Average	4	5 Excellent
...analyzes use of light and color					
...analyzes use of space and composition					
...strength of first iconographic element choice and interpretation					
...strength of second iconographic element choice and interpretation					
...strength of third iconographic element choice and interpretation					
...strength of fourth iconographic element choice and interpretation					
...conclusion regarding story					
Total points					

Sample explanation of values:

Analysis:
- Excellent answer will reflect correct and complete analysis of the ideas.
- Average answer will reflect some but not all of the ideas.
- Poor answer will have little correct information about the ideas.

Figure 5 Grading Rubric

The Pedagogy

The NGen revision of Art History survey II is, as mentioned earlier, composed of seven, two-week modules, each of which are comprised of the same components: lectures, online and other out of class activities, small group work, and the PBL-inspired challenge.

Lectures

There are two lectures, both Mondays, in each two-week module. While there has been much criticism of the lecture model, lectures within this course structure are intended to introduce the framework of the course and each of its constituent modules and, more significantly, to provide an opportunity for students to watch a practiced performance of the tasks that they will be asked to perform in each of the modules.[5] The initial lecture offers an introduction to the module, the primary work of art and methodological approach, and demonstrates its application. The following week's lecture offers new forms of complications engaging, for instance, the ramifications of geographical differences, political conflicts, or temporal change. For example, in the first module the first lecture explains the nature of formal and iconographic analysis and interprets Raphael's painting through these lenses, grounding the methodologies in the philosophical traditions of the Renaissance style, namely humanism, offering similar interpretations of other paintings and monuments. The following week's lecture complicates matters by demonstrating the ways that the pictorial constructions of the Italian Renaissance and the philosophical traditions of humanism might be interpreted differently in different geographical and political contexts during the same historical period—the relationships between the pictorial modes of the Renaissance in Rome, Venice, and the Germanic States, as well as the implications of the visual incompatibility—using the example of the Aztecs and the conquering Spaniards.

Online and other out of class activities

Each module has its own online component in which students access wide-ranging and important course information and content. Some of this is practical: Lecture slides are posted in advance of class so that students can take notes

---

[5] See, for instance, Alison King, "From the Sage on the Stage to the Guide on the Side" *College Teaching* 41, no. 1 (1993): 30–5.

next to the images that are then displayed on the screen. Course readings are posted along with reading questions that are required in order to facilitate preparedness for small group work. The methodological framing of each module is explained. The module problem is posted, along with its grading rubric. Links to additional resources are included.

Significantly, the online format can also facilitate different manners of investigating works of art and architecture. For example, the second course module focuses on Versailles, exploring it in terms of the rhetoric of space. Versailles is a complicated site to teach. The grounds are sprawling and the relationships between buildings, gardens, sculptures, groves, and fountains are difficult to discern. In order to assist students in their exploration of the site, the online component of module two includes an interactive map of Versailles. Students are invited to follow the walking tour that Louis XIV constructed for visitors, and are able to click on different stops along the way, then seeing photographs, works of art, film clips, and Google Earth depictions, allowing them to study the individual stop in more detail but also to consider the relationship between stops in the trajectory of the tour. The experiential aspect of this online element is not simply supplemental to the course material. Instead it allows students to think about the role of time and space in the rhetoric of a site. This is especially important because in this module's problem students are required to come up with their own walking tour and map for a local university campus. In order to create this walking tour, students are required to go to the other university's campus. Throughout the course, site visits to local public monuments and explorations of local museums provide students with the opportunity to solve real-life problems within the discipline of art history.

Small group work

In addition to assimilating the content from lecture and readings, students work through reading questions, and have the opportunity to test out their problem-solving capabilities in collective efforts in a small-group environment prior to their own individual completion of the module problem. The small group offers an opportunity for discussion, questions, and clarification from the instructor or Teaching Assistant in charge of that session. The time is organized in order to provide practice in application of the skills required for the solution of each individual module problem. For example, in the first module, which concerns formal and iconographic analysis within the period style of the Italian Renaissance, students are given paintings to analyze, working together in groups of approximately five. They work together and then present their findings orally to the other three groups in the session. These are graded on a rubric based on the evidence of having completed readings, the quality of their application of the lecture and readings, and their participation in the process. They receive both a grade and oral feedback from the instructor or Teaching Assistant in charge of the session.

PBL-inspired challenge

The PBL-inspired challenges, or problems, require the students to work through real-world applications of art historical methodologies. In this first module this entails formally and iconographically analyzing an unknown work of art. In the third module students propose a Neoclassical history painting to be purchased by one of the local art museums. Students need to prepare a proposal for its acquisition that explains the style, genre, and significance of the selected work, but also contextualizes it within the current collection of paintings on display. In these two examples, students are doing the real work of art historians— whether it be in the auction house or the museum—and utilizing the skills taught in the class, rather than describing them or completing an exam that asks for merely artist, title, and date.

Results

Art History Survey II is offered in only one long semester per year and then once in the shorter summer session. Because of this, it is difficult to assess the relative success or failure of the course by traditional means—there is simply no consistent control group to use for comparison. We do, however, have quantitative data on three different instances of the course – Spring 2007, before the redesign – and Spring 2008 and Spring 2009 with the NGen format. In the last time that the course was taught prior to the redesign, 81% of students enrolled successfully completed the course. In the two iterations of the NGen format, successful completion rates were 82% and 85%. These are not statistically significant differences. This, in itself, however, is significant. The revised course requires more of students—both in terms of higher-order thinking and in sheer numbers of assignments. Yet, despite the added difficultly, students are succeeding at much the same rates. Students similarly evaluated the redesigned course through the department student evaluation form at roughly the same rate as they did the traditional delivery.

On a five-point scale, the traditional course scored 4.49. The first year of the redesign saw the score dip slightly to 3.91 and the second year saw the evaluation score rebound to 4.13.[6]

Sustainability and replication

The redesign of Art History Survey II was intended to be flexible. While thus far it has been taught only by one of the co-designers, it would be possible to hand off the course, with fully-scripted lectures, assignments, online content and interactive multimedia, and grading rubrics, to another instructor. The instructor could then choose to teach the course as it has been created or take the course structure and insert different primary objects or different methodological approaches as suits the instructor's area of specialization or methodological predilection. Depending upon the extent of the alteration, assignments might be either retained or reworked. For instance, a sculptural example, such as Michelangelo's *David* (1504), or an architectural example, such as Bramante's *Tempietto* (1502–10) might take the place of Raphael's *School of Athens* in the first module. It would be possible to retain Versailles in the second module and focus on style or function rather than spatial rhetoric. Similarly the module Impressionism and Realism could be refocused onto Russian Constructivism. Although the instructor would need substantial time to author the changes and insert them into the existing framework, they would have no effect on either the overarching structure of the course or its intended outcomes.

Other issues affecting replicability are room availability and Teaching Assistant preparation. University space allocation systems are notoriously inflexible and securing rooms for the break-out sessions is a challenge each time the class is offered. Should the university's space become more fully subscribed, the redesigned class will risk not having classroom space for the small group meetings. Additionally, as a terminal master's degree program, the pool of available Teaching Assistants prepared to take a leadership role in this type of class is sometimes difficult. Doctoral programs would likely have greater interest from

---

[6] Student opinion polls, as they are called in our college, ask students to rate instructor competence, organization, knowledge level, and other characteristics. In reality, the polls are used by the students to assess both the instructor and the course, as written comments frequently address not just the quality of instruction, but the entire course. It should be noted that the second year of the redesign coincided with a revised student evaluation form with thirteen questions, resulting in lower mean numbers.

potential Teaching Assistants. Our experience has nevertheless shown that even a reticent graduate student, with proper mentoring and guidance, can rise to the challenge of leading undergraduates in discussion and small group activities.

Finally, the cost of the course affects the ability of other art history programs to repeat our efforts. The redesign process was supported by a grant from the university. The initial funds compensated the two authors for our time and paid for supplies and two research assistants who helped us to develop the course materials. Each time the course is taught, the department incurs the cost of the instructor and the three teaching assistants, exactly as with the traditional course. The department additionally gives the course access to an additional graduate student assistant who steps in when the instructor or a teaching assistant is absent in order to maintain the lecture and small-group session schedule. The result is that the course costs little more than it did prior to the redesign, a key goal of the NGen project. That said, the class places higher demands on the teaching assistants compared to other classes and realistically would benefit immensely from more ample staffing; the department lacks funds to provide it.

The N-Gen Process

The N-Gen redesign process is predicated upon a model of a community of practice. The course itself also provides a site of pedagogical apprenticeship for the Teaching Assistants. Indeed, other than presenting the lectures, the Teaching Assistants and the Instructor share the weekly tasks of the course—leading discussion sections, assessing them, and grading written assignments. Significantly, however, in the course of the semester, the Teaching Assistants have the possibility of becoming collaborators with the instructor\designer in the course—suggesting alterations in grading rubrics, texts, and even assignments. In this manner, the undergraduate and graduate students alike are developing their art historical skills. Yet the process is time consuming for the instructor and Teaching Assistants alike—with three Teaching Assistants who are hired for only 10 hours per week assigned to the class, the burden of grading the work of over 300 students can be onerous. Yet, the redesign process is ongoing in this, as in all, classes. Further work includes finding better balances between the needs of faculty and Teaching Assistants to keep their work within reasonable limits. Within this apprenticeship model it is imperative that faculty model behavior for graduate students, just as they do for undergraduates. While for undergraduates this may include demonstrating an eloquent and well-reasoned analysis within the space of lecture, for the graduates this must also include an enactment of limits and efforts towards work\life balance in the ways that the course as a whole may be understood as an exercise in adaptation of Problem-Based Learning—an ill-structured problem to be sure, but one in whose attempt at a solution much is to be gained.

Dr. Tracey Gau
Instructor, English

Case Study: Redesigning World Literature

Background of redesign

World Literature is a two-semester core-curriculum humanities course with an annual enrollment of approximately 550 students taught in multiple sections by numerous instructors with class sizes ranging from 35–150 per section. The pedagogical approach in these classes is overwhelmingly lecture based, and the problems are predictable at both the classroom level and the departmental level: poor student attendance, poor student preparation, high drop, failure, and withdrawal rates, problems of course drift, inconsistent learning experiences, and inefficient use of faculty effort in course delivery. In short, classes like these do not meet university or departmental objectives, and certainly they do not meet the needs of and objectives of students.

Synopsis of redesigned course

In the NGen World Literature courses, students receive a grounding in the content via lecture, practice with the material online, and then meet in smaller groups for interactive discussions. These classes have more small-group discussions and fewer large lectures; they have students actively engaged in online course work, using easy-to-reference online materials; they incorporate activities that require experiential and engaged learning. All efforts work toward increasing the engagement of the student, developing higher-level learning skills, and improving the success rates. This combination of face-to-face and online learning involves students in all facets of cognitive complexity in order to integrate a higher level of critical thinking into the course and to improve success and retention rates that can be measured with reliability and validity.

My approach to the redesign of a literature course is to combine the best practices of traditional pedagogical methodology with the advantages that technology has to offer. The idea is not to replace the content; in fact, the redesigned course materials for the World Literature courses supplement a traditional textbook (the *Norton Anthology of World Literature*). Instead, my efforts are to use technology to move students into a process of internalizing—not memorizing—the material, of experiencing the literature by interacting with it and by relating it to their own lives and experiences. In combining tradition with technology, I aim to overcome some of the problems of the traditional large-enrollment lecture course.

Students meet face-to-face approximately 15 times per semester: 6 large-group lectures (about 8 contact hours), 3 major exams (4 contact hours), and 6 small-group discussions (about 8 contact hours). In each lecture meeting, the instructor introduces three selected texts from the period and focuses on one of those. Usually, two shorter works are paired with a longer one, so that students can work on the shorter works online while rotating through group discussions of the major work. After the introductory lecture, which also models ways of approaching the texts, students begin the sequence of rotating through small-group discussion sessions. In a large class of 150 students, I break the students into 3 groups of 50; in a medium-size class of 60–70 students, I use 2 groups of 30–35. Before coming to their assigned small-group discussion session, students are expected to complete the online materials relating to that text. Additionally, when not in lecture or small group, students complete the online modules for the other two assigned texts. The media-rich, interactive online component of the course replaces the remaining 20–25 of the 45 contact hours.

Creating the foundation

The foundation of an NGen course is an outcomes-based assessment plan that coordinates student learning outcomes, instruction, and assessment items to ensure that what is measured is what is valued. I began the redesign process by creating a course Blueprint or Assessment Plan to ensure that outcomes, lessons, and assessments are aligned. For World Literature, I developed a three-tiered structure that aligns outcomes and assessments—beginning with the large course goals down to the specific lesson outcomes for each major learning module. The three levels are *Institutional, Departmental, and Classroom*. The overall course goals at the Institutional Level set the standard for academic effectiveness; in other words, the four overarching, primary outcomes for World Literature meet university standards and expectations for students taking a World Literature course at UNT. The Departmental Level outcomes then provide a strategic plan for accomplishing each of those overarching course goals; in other words, the outcomes at the Departmental Level make specific how students can achieve the course goals when taking a World Literature course in the Department of English at UNT. Finally, the Classroom Outcomes comprise the pedagogical arena in which students demonstrate the degree to which they have been successful in meeting the expectations set; so, by meeting these classroom outcomes, a student taking Dr. Gau's World Literature course in the Department of English at the University of North Texas effectively meets the expectations of the lesson, the department, and the institution. See http:\\NGen.unt.edu\go\BookMaterials for an example of the assessment plan for this class.

In addition to outlining the Goals and SLOs, the course blueprint or assessment plan shows what types of assessment instruments are used to measure each outcome. The first two Course Learning Goals—(1) to demonstrate an awareness and recognition of the scope and variety of works of literature, and (2) to read critically and analytically—are measured through the three unit exams. Each of these in-class unit exams consists of 60 multiple-choice items and five constructed-response items. The multiple-choice items on these summative exams vary in difficulty level, including each of the learning levels—low (literal and factual), medium (interpretive and analytical), high (metacognitive). The five constructed-response items provide an alternative and complementary means of measuring the first two Course Learning Goals. These five short-answer items are all in the difficulty range of medium-to-high. Constructed response is still one of the best means of meaningfully measuring students' ability to both master and apply concepts within authentic contexts.

As well as writing constructed response answers on exams, students are also required to write 500–600 word compositions throughout the course. These writing assignments correlate to Course Learning Goal 3—to construct informed, organized, and coherent written responses to literary texts. The rubric used to evaluate and provide feedback on these papers includes the standard rhetorical elements of thesis, evidence, and organization, but it also adds the element of "significance." Students in this course are encouraged to relate to the characters, situations, and decisions that they encounter in the literature. In their papers, they must show how what they read is relevant to their own lives. The rubric and a sample composition, with roll-over interactions, are made available to the students via the homepage of the course. See http:\\NGen.unt.edu\go\BookMaterials for the constructed response grading rubric.

Each of these assessment tools begins with and is founded upon measurable learning outcomes. The course blueprint outlines three levels of outcomes—institutional, departmental, and classroom—to ensure the reciprocity of the objectives from the macro to the micro levels. On the micro level, each lesson begins with a set of lesson outcomes, each outcome has an activity that allows the student to practice achieving that outcome, and each outcome is assessed using one or more of these measurements.

The Pedagogy

The course is comprised of lesson modules that begin with outcomes for each and every assigned reading. Each lesson begins with a set of measurable lesson outcomes, progresses into online learning activities and interactions that move students through the readings and prepare them for small-group face-to-face meetings in which they will debate, discuss, collaborate, and present on the material, and finally ends with an assessment that will measure how well students meet the stated lesson outcomes. This recursive process employs a specific mix of lecture, online, and small-group learning strategies at their most efficient and engaging possibilities.

Lecture

The mix of delivery formats in the NGen courses is a deliberate strategy of redesign. I believe that students still need to hear a seasoned expert in the discipline model approaches to the material and offer means to become involved in academic controversy surrounding it. Furthermore, since the sophomore-level World Literature survey courses are intended to introduce students to the discipline at large, the lectures become the most powerful arena to create interest, excitement, and motivation for students—those who may become majors and those who will remain non-majors. Since I place an outline of the notes online, I must do more in lecture periods than simply rehearse them. Having a significant online portion embedded within the course puts additional pressure on the instructor to do more in the lecture. Students will not attend if they do not see value in doing so. Therefore, I use the lecture periods to model various means of interpreting and analyzing literature. Early in the semester, I might lead the class carefully through "reading" questions that form the basis of analysis to model the approach they need to use when on their own. Later, when they meet in small groups, they are then prepared for "discussion" questions that move them into drawing conclusions based on their reading, analysis, and interpretation. Lecture is also a place to synthesize—the historical, geographical, or literary context; to clarify—a particularly challenging reading; to expand—a small but significant excerpt. Last but not least, lecture provides the forum for reassuring students that what they are studying is relevant—not just academically but personally, ethically, relationally.

Online

The purpose of the online components within the course is to provide practical and participatory ways for the students to actively engage with the reading material by fostering a self-administered, creative, and productive means for students to gauge their own understanding and mastery of the assigned material BEFORE coming to class. Each lesson module begins with a set of outcomes that range from from low-level (*identify*) to meduium (*relate*) to high (*analyze*), and each outcome is linked to an activity, either online or in-class, that allows the student to practice mastering that particular outcome. For example, in the Renaissance unit, students can play an online game entitled "Iago's Machiavellianism" in order to identify and relate Machiavellian traits that are exhibited by Iago in William Shakespeare's *Othello*. The online game works like a "reverse" puzzle, in that as the student correctly answers a question from each puzzle piece, the puzzle piece will disappear revealing a piece of an image underneath (See Figure 6.)

This game appears simple, but it requires students to first identify a specific trait then apply it, moving them up the scale of difficulty in an environment that is familiar and non-threatening. These types of formative games and activities are low-stakes assessment strategies that build the student's confidence in their ability to master the material. The result is that students who feel confident with the material at the lower level are prepared to actively engage and participate at higher levels of learning.

Experiential small-group learning

After students have completed the online activities that help them master the material at the literal, factual level, they move to the second step in the learning process: small-group discussions. Once students have completed the online components, they are prepared to come to small-group discussions ready to debate, present, and otherwise actively participate in higher-level learning.

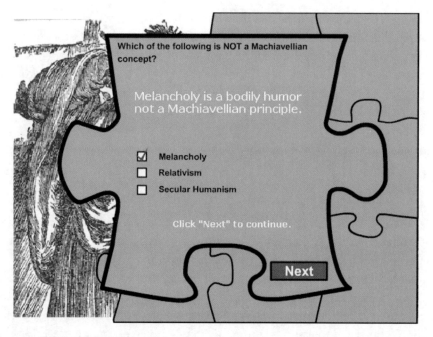

Figure 6 Online Iago Puzzle Game

In addition to increasing student interaction and developing higher-level learning skills, the online components of the course design also appeal to a variety of learning styles and achieve more effective use of classroom time.

One of my most successful small-group assignments is the "Authorship Debate" that preceeds the reading of a Shakespearean play. This assignment requires students to read about a current controversy: who is the author of Shakespeare's plays? They read current articles, each of which builds a case for a particular candidate. When the students come to small-group discussion, they are randomly assigned a candidate, for whom they must present evidence and defend against objections as the author of the plays. The stage is set for a real, live debate with informed and active participants. After the debate, students are asked to abandon their assigned roles and discuss what conclusions they have reached through the process. This collaborative debate does not require students to meet outside of class; instead, it sets the expectation that coming to class prepared is not only essential, it is also exciting, relevant, and worthwhile. One danger of the blended learning environment is that students may adopt the attitude that they don't need to come to class. Therefore, face-to-face time must be readily applicable and germane—to the course and to student lives and experiences. Furthermore, interactive and collaborative activities like these provide tangible, even measurable, evidence of engagement at higher levels of learning. See http:\\NGen.unt.edu\go\BookMaterials for a video clip of the students conducting the Authorship Debate.

Results

To measure the degree to which students meet the stated learning outcomes, the NGen literature courses use four types of assessment: **formative** (low-states mastery quizzes and games), **summative** (in-class unit exams), **constructed response** (compositions and essays on summative exams), and **surveys**. The success rates (students who earn a grade of A, B, or C) of students in the redesigned sections of this course are also compared to those from those of sections taught before the class was redesigned. This comparison is made with the caveat that grades in the non-redesigned sections were not tied to learning outcomes and with the recognition that the redesigned course requires higher level learning.

Summative Exams

The redesigned class was first offered in the fall of 2007. Summative exam scores averaged 78.75 for Goal 1 and 71.67 for Goal 2. NOTE: Goal 2 assessment contained significantly more higher level test items than Goal 1. The assessment results were used to modify the redesign for the spring, 2008 semester.

The summative exam scores for the spring semester showed an improvement over the solid scores from the fall, averaging 86.17 for Goal 1 and 78.67 for Goal 2. See http:\\NGen.unt.edu\go\BookMaterials for detailed information on exam results as well as number of items per goal and cognitive level difficulty.

Surveys

Three surveys are used in the NGen World Literature courses to encourage student critical reflection and analysis of course content and format and to measure student attitudes, perceptions, appreciation, and competency:

1. Survey of Student Attitude Toward Subject
2. Survey of Student Perceptions about Literature
3. Survey of Student Preference: Redesigned vs. Face-to-face Format

These surveys are discussed in detail in Chapter Four.

For the Spring 2008 semester, a statistically significant difference (.05) between pre and post was found on the following questions, indicating an increase in positive opinions toward the course:

- +.33   I like this subject
- +.36   Knowing this subject makes me more employable
- +.23   This subject should be required for all students
- +.54   I know a lot about this subject
- +.33   This subject is relevant to my personal goals

Similarly, a statistically significant difference between pre and post was found on these negatively worded questions, indicating that negative opinions toward the course were reduced:

- −.23   This is a difficult subject for me
- −.49   Learning this subject requires a lot of hard work
- −.29   This subject is difficult to understand
- −.42   I am scared by this subject

Any professor of English would be rewarded to know that students find the study of literature useful, relevant, and worthwhile.

2. The Survey of Student Perceptions about Literature is administered at the end of the semester only and is designed to gather information about how students perceived the degree to which they improved or increased their skills in three main areas: Competency, Critical and Evaluative Thinking, and Appreciation of Literature. The final five questions address instructional design. Students were asked to indicate the degree to which certain course experiences were beneficial to their learning using the same 4-point scale: 1=Very Little; 2=Somewhat; 3=A Good Deal; 4=A Great Deal. The most effective results occurred in the section on the instructional design of the Redesigned course:

- The blended learning format for this course helped with my personal scheduling needs
- The online exercises aided in my learning the material
- The small group discussions aided in my understanding of the material
- Maintaining the same group increased my ability to participate in online and class discussions
- The blended learning format helped me to succeed in this class

COURSE REDESIGN IN PRACTICE: FIVE CASES 109

Students rated each of these aspects as having influenced their success in the course "a good deal." The exception is the penultimate item, which asks about maintaining the same group. According to this survey, students perceive that the smaller group size contributes more to their learning than does having the same members within that group.

Interpreted together, the perception surveys demonstrate that when students are presented with opportunities to master the content at the literal and factual level in an online environment, their fears (of difficulty, applicability, usefulness) are decreased. Furthermore, students perceive that they are better prepared to engage in higher level critical thinking activities, and they more readily see the relevance of the material to personal and professional goals.

3. A final survey administered to students during the last month of the semester asks students about their preference for course format—Redesigned (Blended) vs. Face-to-face (Traditional)—using the following question:

> *If you were to start this course over again, would you prefer a traditional face-to-face format, or would you prefer the N-Gen redesign format you are experiencing? Please tell why.*

The results show that a significantly higher percentage of students (70%) preferred a Redesigned course format versus a traditional, face-to-face (FTF) course format (30%). Additionally, the data show that a significantly higher percentage of successful students (earning grades of A, B, or C) preferred the Redesigned course format (69%) than unsuccessful students. A higher percentage of the unsuccessful students (earning grades of D or F) also preferred the Redesign courses (70%).

Student comments as to why they preferred the redesigned, blended format versus a traditional FTF format were also collected and categorized by the primary reasons for the student's choice. There emerged four reason-categories for the Redesigned format and four for the FTF format. For the Redesigned course format, the reasons fell into the following categories:

1. Pace (liked that they could control the rate at which they absorbed information);
2. Flexibility (liked that they could do assignments whenever and wherever they wanted);
3. Learning (found it easier to learn content when it is internet based);
4. Practice (there were more opportunities to practice and learn).

For the traditional FTF course format, the reasons fell into the following categories:

1. Manage (the need for structure so as not to procrastinate);
2. Learning (found it easier to learn content when format is FTF);
3. People (a preference for face-to-face interactions);
4. Technical (difficulties with computers, network, and technology used).

DFW Rates and Costs

Student perceptions as revealed in the survey and comment data are also verified by the Drop\Failure\Withdrawal (DFW) rates. Over the past 3 years, my two large-enrollment sections of World Literature I courses averaged a DFW rate of 34%. For the first implementation semester of the Redesigned course, Fall 2007, the DFW rate was 29% across sections 001 and 002 of the course, a decrease of 5%. At the end of the second implementation semester, Spring 2008, the DFW decreased to 16%.

It is notable that higher level cognitive items are included in the summative assessment vehicles in the redesigned sections. These items are written to match the intent of the redesigned student learning outcome statements. Previous course administrations did not include these higher level outcomes and items. Thus, a 16% reduction may indicate a more effective use of resources—for students, instructors, and the university. The increased success rates of the two course sections also may indicate that the strategies of moving toward experiential, student-centered, and active learning that emphasize analysis, synthesis, and application are having a significantly positive impact on student learning.

Overall, the assessment results show that the blended course design addresses the problems of poor attitudes, lack of preparation, high DFW rates, and low-level, passive learning through memorization, and transforms the classroom into a discovery-based, student-led place of active and experiential learning that is built around interaction with the primary materials.

The cost of instruction in terms of successful (Grade of A, B, or C) and highly successful (Grade of A or B) can be compared between the traditional and redesigned version of the course. However, since the Student Learning Outcomes in the redesigned course were at a higher level, the very nature of "success" lends a cautionary tone to this comparison. Based upon the five semesters of teaching World Literature (two traditional and three redesign, the cost of instruction in the traditional class was $79 per successful student and

$105 per highly successful student. For the redesign, with more challenging Student Learning Outcomes, the costs were $68 and $86 respectively.

Sustainability and replication

As the instructor leading the redesign of World Literature, I have continued to improve the redesign each time I have taught the course. In addition, the redesign is meant to enable other faculty to use the redesign approach as adapted to meet their teaching style. The NGen World Literature courses offer enough of a variety of texts that instructors can choose which ones to include or exclude. However, a "buffet" approach is not the goal: the courses are deliberately constructed to have outcomes, activities, and assessments integrated together. Instructors who have taught the NGen literature courses create their own syllabus, assignments, and can select precisely which activities to include in each and every lesson module. This kind of freedom of choices and of making changes is embedded within the design. Of course, this extent of flexibility means that as a designer I must constantly and consistently revise, edit, and add to the course.

The N-Gen Process

In addition to engaging students at higher levels, increasing the effectiveness of student learning, and reviving my own pedagogical methods, designing and teaching a blended course through the N-Gen process have also led to other unexpected benefits. The redesigned course materials and pedagogical approach offer a solid context from which to introduce graduate teaching fellows to the teaching of literature. Graduate assistants may begin by grading online discussion posts and compositions, then move into using the curriculum materials created during the redesign process to lead some of the small-group discussions and sessions. In effect, the instructor models the best practices of aligning measurable objectives, activities, and assessments, of using technology in meaningful ways, and of increasing student interaction—all while maintaining academic rigor, integrity, and freedom.

The N-Gen redesign process establishes, develops, and continually nurtures a Community of Practice that is integral to the redesign process. In this interdisciplinary community, we come together each month to share ideas and methodologies, to test out new assignments (both online and group), and to learn about new technologies and processes of blended learning. My teams have benefited in particular from the participation of the Senior Faculty Fellows who have redesigned courses in the past. We learn from their successes and mistakes—in both design and implementation—and can use their examples as springboards in our own course development.

However, beyond the small circle of innovators, course redesign faces formidable challenges. Primarily, faculty, department chairs, administrators, and even publishers are hesitant to take risks. A lack of rewards for the effort, expertise, and innovation of course development is clearly an obstacle for faculty who are interested in redesign but do not consider the risk worth the reward in an environment where research and publication take precedent. Secondly, there is a distinct hostility to change, often and especially in one's own department, which affects whether anyone is willing to adopt and use the redesigned course. Faculty often resist change because they are entrenched in a comfortable pedagogy, and department chairs are often reluctant to assign faculty to teach the blended versions, preferring a wait-and-see approach.

To address these challenges, we need to nurture continued interdisciplinary communities of practice, create a culture of reflection among faculty involved in and interested in redesign, and respond to student demand for change. We need to work to change the recognition and reward system through the creation of a professional career track for instructors, the development of institution-wide teaching assessment, and the revision of workload documents. The creation of courses that emphasize problem solving and critical thinking, and that incorporate active and experiential learning components, measureable student learning outcomes, and valid assessment (results that can be generalized beyond the particular course section) is essential in today's universities.

Dr. Kelly McMichael
Associate Director, Center for Learning Enhancement, Assessment, and Redesign and Instructor, History

Case Study: Redesigning U.S. History

Background of redesign

The United States History course is a survey required of all students in the state of Texas. It is traditionally taught using a lecture format with three or four non-comprehensive exams. Students have few opportunities to engage directly with the content, primary sources, each other, or the faculty member. At UNT, this course is taught in the large-enrollment format with between 125 and 300 students in each section.

Synopsis of redesigned course

I spent a year redesigning the U.S. History I survey and developing the curriculum materials. I kept three primary objectives in mind when I began the N-Gen redesign process:

1. Students will learn the basic facts and chronology of U.S. History.
2. Students will engage directly with primary sources, applying them to solve historical problems in a real-world and relevant context.
3. Students will increase interest and motivation in U.S. History and they will become life-long learners of history.

It seemed to me that the course had stressed facts and chronology at the expense of application, giving students a false sense of what historians actually do. I wanted to correct this by emphasizing the interpretative nature of the discipline. I knew that to achieve this goal, I would have to find specific historical problems for the students to engage in that would hold their interest but also serve as microcosms for the broader themes they needed to learn.

To meet these main objectives, the redesigned course has a two-part format:

1. *Students learn the facts and chronology of U.S. History through interactive, media-rich online lessons.* Each lesson is based on mastery learning so that students cannot move to the next lesson until they have achieved a faculty-set standard. Online content includes a comprehensive midterm and final exam.
2. *Students engage directly with primary sources, applying them to solve historical problems in a real-world and relevant context.* Students work on case studies (implemented as role-playing simulations) that highlight specific historical content in a problem-based format.

The students work on the online portion of the class independently on their own and come to class to engage in the role-playing simulations. I believe this format gives them both a broad over-view of the time period, which is what they normally receive in the survey, but also provides them with an in-depth exploration into particular topics. Students are rarely afforded a deep look at a historical situation in the survey course because there are always too many topics to cover. I "bought" time for a deep probe by eliminating the lecture component and replacing it with online materials.

Creating the foundation: Student learning outcomes and assessment

The foundation of the U.S. History I Survey lies within the Student Learning Outcomes (SLOs). The SLOs for this course are descriptions of the measurable behaviors and products that I expect from students as a result of my instruction and their learning. In other words, learning outcomes are what students *are expected to be able to do* after being taught. The following is an example of one of our Student Learning Outcomes in the course:

> Goal 2: The student will understand how early European exploration and colonization resulted in cultural and ecological interactions among previously unconnected peoples.
>
>> Objective 1: Student understands the stages of European oceanic and overland exploration, amid international rivalries, from the 9th to 17th centuries by
>>
>>> Outcome 1: Identifying and analyzing routes taken by early explorers, from the 15th through the 17th century, around Africa, to the Americas, and across the Pacific.
>>>
>>> Outcome 2: Evaluating the significance of Columbus' voyages and his interactions with indigenous peoples.
>>>
>>> Outcome 3: Comparing and making generalizations about the English, French, and Dutch motives for exploration with those of the Spanish.
>>>
>>> Outcome 4: Identifying, analyzing and evaluating the course and consequences of the "Biological Exchange."
>>
>> Objective 2: Student understands the Spanish and Portuguese conquest of the Americas by
>>
>>> Outcome 1: comparing the various motives of the Spanish and Portuguese for exploration and colonization.
>>>
>>> Outcome 2: evaluating the Spanish interactions with such people as Aztecs, Incas, and Pueblos.

Once I had written my outcomes, I matched them with assessments so that student learning could be measured. Once measured, I would then be able to make meaningful decisions about the kinds of learning that had occurred in the class and adjust my teaching practices, if needed. I use a course blueprint to visually represent my course SLOs and assessments. See http:\\NGen.unt.edu\go\BookMaterials for a sample of the course blueprint for this course.

Assessments for this course included lesson mastery multiple-choice quizzes, a multiple-choice midterm and final exam. For the case studies, written papers and speeches, oral performances, and online discussion board postings were used. The constructed responses, oral performance pieces, and discussion posts are evaluated using rubrics, which are given to the students along with the assignments. See examples of the rubrics at http:\\NGen.unt.edu\go\BookMaterials.

The Pedagogy

Lecture

There is no lecture in the redesigned course. Instead, the in-class portion of the course consists of role-playing simulations played by the students. I generally use four simulations—one to anchor each of the course units. This is the heart of the class and reflects the move to "active learning." The simulations I have used that students like best are:

- CSI: Philip Nolan
- La Amistad: Revolt for Freedom
- The Politics of Manifest Destiny
- The Texas Troubles

The students are assigned specific roles to play in the simulations. They are then divided into factions based on those roles so that they can work collaboratively. They must use primary source documents to prepare for their roles, and they work outside of class within their factions to prepare for the in-class role-playing.

For example, the case study "The Politics of Manifest Destiny," is based on the counter-factual premise that the popularly-elected Texas Constitutional Convention, along with specific guests, gathered in June of 1845 to vote on two specific issues:

- to accept an offer of peace from the Mexican government, possibly ending hostilities between the two nations or
- to accept an annexation proposal from the United States, bringing an end to the Republic of Texas.

See Figure 7 for a photo of students playing simulation game.

Figure 7 Students Playing Simulation Game

The "guests" joining the convention members include former Texas Presidents Sam Houston and Mirabeau Lamar, Benjamin Lundy, Ashbel Smith, John Tyler, James K. Polk, Felix Huston, and a Comanche Chief. In reality, the Convention gathered to consider the proposal of annexation put forward by the United States, as well as a proposed peace treaty with Mexico. Once the convention accepted the annexation proposal, the proposal moved on to a popular vote held in October 1845. The game eliminates the popular vote and assumes that the members of the Constitutional Convention were representing specific constituents, had the power to vote on the two bills proposed, and that the vote would determine the legal outcome.

Students are given specific roles to play. There are nine roles that represent the key issues involved in making the decision to either vote for or against annexation. These roles represent the key players in the case study. All other students play "indeterminates." The indeterminates are students who have primary and secondary objectives but who are undecided on the issue of annexation.

The active role-playing aspects of this simulation take place at the Caucus and Convention session. As President of the Republic of Texas, the student-playing Anson Jones runs the Caucus and Convention session. Jones calls for the caucuses to convene and organizes the format of the session. While Jones establishes the general rules of the proceedings, he also must decide how he will vote, along with the other indeterminates. The case study facilitator (the instructor) informs Jones of his responsibilities and then allows him to take control of the proceedings.

The instructor (called the case study facilitator during the role-playing portion of the simulation) organizes the case study simulation by dividing the students into their roles and providing a mini-lecture to ground the case study in its period, providing background and context for the students.

The instructor establishes the case study rules (assignments, due dates, discussion boards) and assists the students in preparing for the caucus and convention sessions. The instructor may also allow some in-class time for students to organize themselves.

During the caucus and convention session, the instructor literally and figuratively moves to the side. Anson Jones runs the class, determining the order of the caucus activities and session, and makes all major decisions. The students may call upon the instructor to clarify a fact. The instructor can insert a comment but should keep it brief so that the students remain in control.

Once the role-playing simulation process has finished, the instructor holds a reflection session. During this time, the instructor briefs the students about what actually happened in the past and illustrates how the students' decisions and arguments were different from the ones actually made. The instructor encourages students to talk about their roles and the parts that they played, making the "larger" connections to the broad scope of United States History. They also discuss how their engagement in the simulation illustrates the interpretive nature of the discipline. Most students find it difficult to understand that History is not a series of names, dates, or "right" answers. The reflective session provides a perfect opportunity for the instructor to get into this element of higher-order thinking.

The students are graded individually for their work in the role-playing simulation even though they work collaboratively during the preparation and play time. Each student writes two papers: one is a speech to be delivered at either the caucus or the convention and the other is a reflective paper completed at the end of the course. In addition to the two papers, each student is required to post materials online in their factions. These postings might include speeches, primary documents, thoughts, or strategies. The online postings have varied but have most often been on the discussion board of a learning management system, on a wiki, or on an open-sourced social networking site. The final component of a student's grade is oral performance. Because these case studies are conducted as role-playing simulations, the students are speaking in public. Each student receives an oral performance grade, based mostly on participation and preparation.

Online

The online course materials consist of 15 media-rich lessons anchored by a mastery-based quiz. Each lesson contains text, images, video, audio, and flash-based learning objects created in an attempt to address varying student learning styles. See Figure 8 for screen shot of online materials.

The lessons include:

- **Unit 1** Colliding Cultures

    Lesson 1: Pre-Columbian America
    Lesson 2: European Exploration and Colonization of the New World
    Lesson 3: The New World and the Old
    Lesson 4: The Colonial Experiment

- **Unit 2** Colonization and Revolution

    Lesson 5: The English Empire
    Lesson 6: The Revolution
    Lesson 7: Creating the United States
    Lesson 8: Change of Power

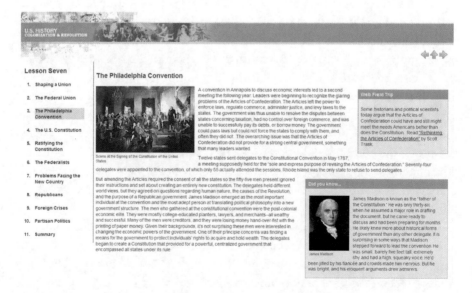

Figure 8 Online U.S. History Content

- **Unit 3** A New Nation Emerging

    Lesson 9: The Growing Nation
    Lesson 10: Rise in Democracy
    Lesson 11: American Society and Culture
    Lesson 12: Manifest Destiny

- **Unit 4** A Country Dividing

    Lesson 13: A House Dividing
    Lesson 14: Civil War
    Lesson 15: Reconstruction

Results

The following data is taken from a Fall 2007 pilot of the course materials at the University of North Texas. The same instructor taught the pilot of the course and the control group (comparison class). I was not the instructor in these courses, meaning that we wanted to see how effective someone else could be teaching with this pedagogical approach.

U.S. History I:

Enrollment: 212 pilot versus 122 comparative
Completion: 208 pilot versus 118 comparative

Success Rates in two courses taught by same instructor

Pilot Course: 87%
Traditional Course: 56%

Failure rates in two courses taught by same instructor

Pilot Course: 13%
Traditional Course: 44%

Success rates of pilot compared with ALL large enrollment (150+) sections taught at UNT:

Pilot Course: 87%
Traditional Course: 64%

Percent students taking the redesign course who preferred the redesign format over traditional Lecture in U.S. History 1301

Pilot Course: 57%
Traditional Course: 39%

The following are student comments from a survey taken mid-semester about the course pedagogical approach:

> "At first when I found out what this class was I was a little upset and annoyed because I felt confused by the first game and I felt it would be easier to just listen to a lecture and take notes. True it might have been easier to listen (or day dream) through a lecture, but would I have learned as much? In reality I probably did learn more through the mixed course than I would've memorizing facts for a test that I would have forgotten the next day anyway. This class proved a fun and entertaining way to learn. The papers were a bit of a hassle at times, but I got them done. I always forgot about the quizzes though. There should be more in-class reminders on those."

> "I would prefer a face to face format because I am the type of person who needs set rules and regulations. With taking quizzes and writing papers and posting discussions online, I constantly forget to do them because I am not used to doing everything on the internet. Whenever we do not have class time, I consider that time free time and not time to do work."

> "N-Gen Redesign. I think it worked better\easier for interaction. Face to face class tends to be boring and being able to do most of the work online saves time and makes it easier for me to learn. I feel I actually learn more rather than just memorizing information for a test."

Sustainability and replication

The greatest challenge I faced in implementing problem-based learning in my course involved the sheer number of students in a single class section. I knew that I needed to break the students into small groups and meet with the groups individually but that is a challenge when there is only one instructor and one teaching assistant.

The first semester that I taught the redesigned course I had 125 students, and I broke them into five groups of 25 students. The student groups rotated into class once every two weeks to engage in the role-playing simulations. I was in the classroom on Monday, Wednesday, and Friday, but each group was assigned a "class day" and only came to class the one time, every other week. While this system allowed me to meet with each small group individually, it proved inadequate because two-week intervals between f2f meetings caused the students to lose momentum in the role-playing simulations.

Since the initial semester, I have changed the format so that each group of students comes to class once a week. This has improved the feelings of cohesiveness within the simulations and has given the course greater unity. I have accomplished this by training the teaching assistant to facilitate small groups, allowing for more than one group to meet at a time.

I have since modified the course structure so that an even larger section of students can be taught using this method. This is an example of human resource reallocation within the college paradigm. For example in this format, 220 students have enrolled in the course section with one instructor of record. The students were then broken into 11 small groups with 20 students in each group. The instructor of record served as a course manager and trained six teaching assistants to facilitate the small group role-playing simulations. Each facilitator had a grader who graded all written assignments based on rubrics. The instructor trained the facilitators and graders, insured quality in the online component, and observed the facilitators during the in-class role-playing simulations.

REFERENCES

Adelman, C. (1999). *Answers in the toolbox: Academic intensity, attendance patterns, and bachelor's degree attainment.* Washington, D.C.: Office of Educational Research and Improvement, U.S. Department of Education.

Association for the Study of Higher Education. (2007). Student behaviors, activities, and experiences associated with student success. *ASHE Higher Education Report, 32*(5), 43–67.

Asmar, C. (2002). Strategies to enhance learning and teaching in a research-extensive university. *International Journal for Academic Development, 7*(1), 18–30.

Australian Universities Teaching Committee . (2003). *Teaching Large Classes Project 2001 Final Report.* Queensland, Australia: The University of Queensland Teaching and Educational Development Institute.

Biggs, J.B. & Collis, K.F. (1982). *Evaluating the quality of learning: the SOLO taxonomy.* New York: Academic Press.

Biggs, J.B. & Tang, C.S. (2007). *Teaching for quality learning at university: what the student does.* Maidenhead, England: McGraw-Hill/Society for Research into Higher Education & Open University Press.

Boyer Commission on Educating Undergraduates in the Research University (1998). *Reinventing Undergraduate Education: a blueprint for America's Research Universities.* Princeton, NJ: Carnegie Foundation for the Advancement of Teaching. (ERIC Document Reproduction Service No. ED424840)

Carriveau, R.S. (2008). *Writing outcome-based assessments handbook.* Denton, TX: Center for Learning Enhancement, Assessment, and Redesign, University of North Texas.

Chickering, A.W. & Gamson, Z.F. (1987). Seven principles for good practice in undergraduate education. *AAHE Bulletin, 39*(7), 3–7.

Coy, P. (2009). What falling prices tell us. *Business Week,* (4119), 24–26.

Erlauer, L. (2003). *The brain-compatible classroom.* Alexandria, VA: Association for Supervision and Curriculum Development.

Freeland, R. (2009). Liberal education and effective practice: The necessary revolution in undergraduate education. *Liberal Education, 95*(1), 6–13.

Gagné, R.M. (1985). *The conditions of learning and theory of instruction.* New York: Holt, Rinehart, and Winston.

Gardner, H.W. (1993). Educating for understanding. *The American School Board Journal, 180*(7), 20–24.

Haladyna, T.M. (1999). *Developing and validating multiple-choice test items* (2nd ed.). Mahwah, NJ: L. Erlbaum Associates.

Hashimshony, R. & Haina, J. (2006). Designing the university of the future. *Planning for Higher Education*, 34(2), 5–19.

Hodge, D, Lepore, P., Pasquesi, K., & Hirsh, M. (2008). Preparing students for research and creative work. *Liberal Education*, 94(3), 6–15.

Hussar, W. & Bailey, T. (2008). *Projections of Educational Statistics to 2017*. Washington, D.C.: National Center for Education Statistics, Institute of Education Sciences, U.S. Department of Education.

Inderbitzin, M. & Storrs, D.A. (2008). Mediating the conflict between transformative pedagogy and bureaucratic practice. *College Teaching*, 56(1), 47–52.

Kegan, R. (1994). *In over our heads: The mental demands of modern life*. Cambridge, MA: Harvard University Press.

Kuh, G., Cruce, T., Shoup, R. Kinzie, J., & Gonyea, r. (2008). Unmasking the effects of student engagement on first-year college grades and persistence. *Journal of Higher Education*, 79(5), 540-563.

Lee, V., Hyman, M., & Luginbuhl, G. (2007). The concept of readiness in the academic department: A case study of undergraduate reform. *Innovative Higher Education*, 32(1), 3–18.

Manwaring, M. (2006). The cognitive demands of a negotiation curriculum: What does it mean to "get" getting to YES? *Negotiation Journal*, 22(1), 67–88.

Mattson, K. (2005). Why "active learning" can be perilous to the profession. *Academe*, 91(1), 23–26.

McLuhan, M. & Fiore, Q. (1967). *The medium is the massage*. New York: Random House.

Means, B., Toyama, Y., Murphy, R., Bakia, M., and Jones, K. (2009). *Evaluation of Evidence-Based Practices in Online Learning: A Meta-Analysis and Review of Online Learning Studies*. Washington, D.C.: Office of Planning, Evaluation, and Policy Development, Policy and Program Studies Service. U.S. Department of Education.

Moore, A.H., Fowler, S.B., & Watson, C.E. (2007). Active learning and technology :Designing change for faculty, students, and institutions. *Educause Review*, 42(5), 42–60.

Moore, W.S. (1990). *The learning environment preferences: An instrument marval*. Olympia: Center for the Study of Intellectual Development.

Osterlind, S.J. (1998). *Constructing test items: multiple-choice, constructed-response, performance, and other formats*. Boston: Kluwer Academic Publishers.

Pardue, K, & Morgan, P. (2008). Millennials considered: A new generation, new approaches and implications for nursing education. *Nursing Education Perspectives*, 29(2), 74–79.

Pascarella, E.T. & Ternzini, P.T. (2005). *How college affect sudents:* (1st ed.) San Francisco: Jossey Bass.

Parini, J. (2005). *The Art of Teaching*. New York: Oxford University Press.

Ramsden, P. (2003). *Learning to teach in higher education*. London: Routledge Falmer.

Reason, R., Terenzini, P., & Domingo, R. (2006). First things first: Developing academic competence in the first year of college. *Research in Higher Education*, 47(2), 149–175.

Rimer, S. (2009, January 13). At MIT, large lectures are going the way of the blackboard. *New York Times*, p. 12.

Seymour, E. & Hewitt, N. (1997). *Talking about leaving: Why undergraduates leave the sciences*. Boulder, CO: Westview Press.

Smith, T.W. & Colby, S.A. (2007). Teaching for Deep Learning. *Clearing House*, 80(5), 205–210.

Tapscott, D. (2008, December 1). "How to Teach and Manage 'Generation Net'." *Business Week Online*, 7. Retrieved January 29, 2009, from https://vpn.unt.edu/+CSCO+ch756767

63663A2F2F79766F6365626B6C2E79766F656E656C2E6861672E7271683A39343433++/login?url=http://search.ebscohost.com/login.aspx?direct=true&db=a9h&AN=35612821&site=ehost-live&scope=site

Tapscott, D. (2009). *Grown up digital.* New York: McGraw Hill.

Turner, P.M. & Riedling, A.M. (2003). *Helping teachers teach: A school library media specialist's role* (3rd ed.). Westport, CT: Libraries Unlimited.

U.S. Department of Education, National Center for Education Statistics. (2006). *Digest of Education Statistics, 2005.* Washington, D.C.: Author.

U.S. Department of Education, National Center for Education Statistics. (2008). *Digest of Education Statistics, 2007.* Washington, D.C.: Author.

Wesch, M. (2007). A vision of students today [Video file]. Video posted to http://www.youtube.com/watch?v=dGCJ46vyR9o

Wieman, C. (2007). Why not try a scientific approach to science education? *Change, 39*(5), 9–15.

Wolfe, P. (2001). *Brain matters: translating research into classroom practice.* Alexandria, VA: Association for Supervision and Curriculum Development.

Zull, J. E. (2002). *The art of changing the brain: enriching teaching by exploring the biology of learning.* Sterling, VA: Stylus.

INDEX

academical village, 65
accountability in higher education, 7
active learning
   in art history course, 90
   in biology course, 70, 73, 74–75
   critical thinking and, 8
   deep learning and, 14
   importance of, 8
   national context of course
      redesign and, 21
   student engagement and, 15
   in U.S. history course, 113, 115–117
   in world literature course, 110
administrative units, 66–67
Adoption of Courseware Survey for
   Faculty Members, 50
affective tests, 42
ambiguity and cognitive development, 16
American government course expceriential
   learning activity, 31–33

art history course redesign
   active learning in, 90
   assessment in, 91–95
   assessment results of, 98–99
   background of, 89
   classroom scheduling of, 99
   Community of Practice and, 100–101
   costs of, 100
   course redesign process and, 100–101
   critical thinking in, 89, 91
   experiential learning in, 97
   lecture-based instruction in, 90, 96
   objectives of, 92–95
   online learning activities in, 96–97
   problem based learning in, 90–91,
      94, 98, 101
   small group work in, 90, 97–98
   sustainability and replication of, 99–100
   synopsis of, 89–91
   teaching assistants in, 99–100

Art of Changing the Brain (Zull), 10
Asmar, C., 61
assessment
  affective tests, 42
  in art history course, 91–95, 98–99
  in biology course, 71–72, 74, 75–77
  cognitive tests, 42
  in communicating in business course, 80–81, 82, 84–86
  costs and, 37, 58
  deep learning and, 14, 44
  definition of, 41–42
  in identifying course problems, 54
  to justify course redesign, 62
  multiple iterations of, 25
  in online environment, 40
  plan, 33, 37–38, 62, 63
  publicity about, 33, 63–64
  purposes of, 43–44
  of redesigned courses and programs, 47–51
  rewarding quality teaching and, 65
  in short term plan, 58
  staff, 28, 35, 60
  of student engagement, 62
  surface learning and, 12
  survey instruments for, 47–51
  training for faculty in, 29, 34–35, 60
  in U.S. history course, 113, 114–115, 117, 118, 119–120
  in world literature course, 102–104, 105, 107–111
  See also goals; surveys
attitude toward subject of course, survey of, 48, 62, 77, 85, 107–108
authority and cognitive development, 16

Baxter, Denise, 89–101
Biggs, J. B., 13
biology course redesign
  active learning in, 70, 73, 74–75
  assessment in, 71–72, 74
  assessment results of, 75–77
  background of, 70
  Community of Practice and, 78
  costs of, 77
  course redesign process and, 78
  lecture-based instruction in, 70, 71, 72, 73
  objectives of, 71, 72
  online learning activities in, 70–71, 73–74
  recitation activities in, 70, 71, 72, 73, 74–75
  small group work in, 70, 74–75
  sustainability and replication of, 77
  synopsis of, 70–71
  teaching assistants in, 77
Blended Learning Projects, 22–24
Boyer Commission on Educating Undergraduates in the Research University, 13
brain and learning, 9–12
business communication course redesign. *See* communicating in business course redesign

calendar for course redesign, 57–58
Carriveau, R. S., 45
change, resistance to, 4, 53, 112
chemistry course redesign activity, 56
Chickering, A. W., 15
classroom scheduling, 53, 55, 58, 63, 64–65, 99
Cognitive Complexity Index, 48
cognitive development, 15–17, 18, 62
cognitive skills, higher level, 35, 49
cognitive tests, 42
Colby, S. A., 14
collaborative learning, 8, 11, 18, 40
  See also small group work
Collis, K. F., 13
communicating in business course redesign
  assessment in, 80–81, 82
  assessment results of, 84–86
  background of, 79
  Community of Practice and, 87–88
  course redesign process and, 87–88
  critical thinking in, 80, 83, 88
  experiential learning in, 80
  lecture-based instruction in, 79, 80, 82–83
  objectives of, 81
  online learning activities in, 80, 84
  small group work in, 80, 82, 83–84, 87
  student engagement in, 79, 80, 82, 84, 85, 86, 87, 88

sustainability and replication of, 86–87
synopsis of, 79–80
team projects in, 80, 81, 82, 83–84, 87
communication channels for publicity, 63–64
Community of Practice
   administrative unit and, 66–67
   in art history course, 100–101
   in biology course, 78
   in communicating in business course, 87–88
   creation of, 59–62
   definition of, 28
   Next Generation Course Redesign Project and, 26, 28
   request for proposal and, 27
   training of faculty and, 35
   in world literature course, 111–112
   See also Faculty Fellows
Community of Practice Survey, 51
constructed response items
   in art history course, 94
   rubrics and, 37, 47
   specific learning outcomes and, 49
   student learning outcomes and, 37, 42
   test specifications plan and, 44, 45
   training in, 35
   in U.S. history course, 117
   validating, 45, 47
   in world literature course, 103, 107
   writing guidelines for, 45
core curriculum (University of North Texas), 89, 92, 101
costs of redesigned courses
   in art history course, 100
   assessment and, 58
   in biology course, 77
   elements affecting, 58–59, 60–62
   goals and, 36
   in world literature course, 110–111
course format survey, 48, 77, 84–85, 109–110
course problems, identification of, 54
course redesign
   assessment of (*See* assessment)
   barriers and challenges to, 53, 88, 112
   calendar for, 57–58
   financial aspects (*See* costs of redesigned courses; funding; grants)
   goals of (*See* goals)

   justifications for, 3–8, 54, 62
   national context of, 21–22
   project leader for, 55
   publicity about, 33, 58, 63–64
   scope of, 55–57
   structure for, 60
   support for, 58–59, 60–62, 88
   See also Next Generation Course Redesign Project
course redesign case studies
   art history course, 89–101
   biology course, 70–78
   communicating in business course, 79–88
   U.S. history course, 112–121
   world literature course, 101–112
course redesign process
   in art history course, 100–101
   in biology course, 78
   in communicating in business course, 87–88
   in world literature course, 111–112
courses, general education. *See* general education courses
course scheduling, 53, 55, 58, 63, 64–65, 99
course sections and redesign considerations, 56–57
courseware production, 59, 66
courseware survey for faculty members, 50
coverage in teaching, 4
critical thinking
   active learning and, 8
   in art history course, 89, 91
   in communicating in business course, 80, 83, 88
   coverage of content in teaching and, 4
   deep learning and, 14
   experiential learning and, 40
   Learning Environment Preferences survey and, 49
   lecture-based instruction and, 8
   student learning outcomes and, 36
   in world literature course, 101, 108, 109, 112
Cross, R., 28

deep learning, 12, 13, 14, 39, 44
demographics and higher education, 6

departmental approach to course redesign, 55–56, 57
development, cognitive, 15–17, 18, 62
digital technology. *See* technology
Domingo, R., 14
Donahue-Wallace, Kelly, 89–101

education, higher. *See* higher education
effective teaching, rewarding of, 65–66
engagement of students. *See* student engagement
enrollment demographics of higher education, 6
Erlauer, L., 11
evaluation. *See* assessment
evaluative skills, measurement of, 49
examinations. *See* assessment
experiential learning
  in American government course, 31–33
  in art history course, 97
  best uses of, 40
  classroom scheduling for, 64–65
  in communicating in business course, 80
  course redesign publicity and, 33, 63
  critical thinking and, 40
  goals of course redesign process and, 25
  involving peers, 11
  national context of course redesign and, 21
  Net Generation students and, 18
  in physics education, 22
  in world literature course, 101, 105–107, 110, 112

faculty
  incentives for, 61–62
  rewards and recognition for, 53, 61, 65–66, 112
  role in the learning process, 10, 12
  training of, 29, 34–35, 60
  workload policy for, 66
  see also Community of Practice; Faculty Fellows
faculty development specialist, 28
Faculty Fellows, 27–35, 59–60
  See also Community of Practice
Faculty Fellows, Senior. *See* Senior Faculty Fellows

financial aspects of course redesign. *See* costs of redesigned courses; funding; grants
financial aspects of higher education, 6–7
Finding the perfect blend (Pearcy, A. G.), 48
format of course, assessment of preferences for, 48, 62, 77, 84–85, 109–110
Freeland, Richard, 21
Frost, Robert, 4
funding, 27, 55, 58–59
  See also grants

Gagne, R. M., 10
Gamson, Z, F, 15
Gardner, H. W., 4
Gau, Tracey, 34, 101–112
general education courses
  cognitive development and, 17
  enrollment demographics and, 6
  higher education finances and, 6
  importance of, 8
  Net Generation students and, 7, 18
  Quality Enhancement Plan and, 24
  redesign of (*See* course redesign)
  success rates in, 5, 54
general outcomes, 43–44
goals
  of art history course, 92–95
  assessment of redesigned courses and, 47–51
  of biology course, 71, 72
  of communicating in business course, 80–81, 86
  costs of redesigned courses and, 36
  of Next Generation Course Redesign Project, 25–26
  of Next Generation courses, 35–36, 42
  outcome statements and, 41–44
  test specifications plan and, 44–45
  of U.S. history course, 113
  validating test items and, 45–47
  of world literature course, 102–104
  See also assessment; general outcomes; student learning outcomes; specific learning outcomes
government course experiential learning activity, 31–33

INDEX

graduate teaching assistants. *See* teaching assistants
grants, 23, 25, 58, 60, 61
See also funding
group work. *See* small group work

Haladyna, T. M., 45
Hewitt, N., 5
higher education
  accountability in, 7
  changes in 20th century, 3–4
  enrollment demographics in, 6
  financial aspects of, 6, 7
  general education course success rates and, 5
higher level cognitive skills, 35, 49
higher level learning
  collaborative work and, 8, 11
  complex neural networks and, 14
  course redesign goals and, 35, 36
  student engagement and, 7
  in world literature course, 101, 105, 106, 107
higher level thinking, 11, 15, 90, 91, 98, 117
Hirsh, M., 17, 21
history (U.S.) course redesign.
  See U.S. history course redesign
Hodge, D., 17, 21
Hugh, Lee, 26
Hughes, Lee, 70–78
Hyman, M., 56

incentives for faculty, 61–62
independent learning, 14
information technology. *See* technology
Insley, Robert G., 79–88
institutional support, 58–59, 60–62, 88
instruction. *See* teaching
instructional consultants, 28, 35
instructors. *See* faculty
intellectual development, measurement of, 48–49
intellectual property policy, 59
interdisciplinary approach to course redesign, 55–56, 57
introductory courses. *See* general education courses

introductory survey courses. *See* general education courses
item analysis, 46–47, 49–50
items, constructed response. *See* constructed response items
items, multiple choice. *See* selected response items
items, selected response. *See* selected response items
items, test. *See* test items

James Madison University Library, 65
Jefferson, Thomas, 65

Kegan, Robert, 16–17, 18
Kuh, G., 14

Laseter, T., 28
leadership enabling course redesign, 55
learner responses, 13
learning
  brain and, 9–12
  cognitive development and, 15–17
  levels of, 12–14
  Net Generation and, 7, 17–19
  social aspects of, 11, 15, 65
  student engagement and, 7, 14–15
  teacher's role in, 10, 12
learning, active. *See* active learning
learning, collaborative. *See* collaborative learning
learning, deep, 12, 13, 14, 39, 44
learning, experiential. *See* experiential learning
learning, higher level. *See* higher level learning
learning, independent, 14
learning, surface. *See* surface learning
Learning Environment Preferences survey, 48–49
lecture-based instruction
  in art history course, 90, 96
  best uses of, 40
  in biology course, 70, 71, 72, 73
  in communicating in business course, 79, 80, 82–83
  critical thinking and, 8
  limitations of, 6–7, 8, 14, 17

pervasiveness of, 3–4
preference for, 63
technology and, 4
in U.S. history course, 114, 115
in world literature course, 101, 102, 104–105
Lee, V., 56
LEP. *See* Learning Environment Preferences survey
Lepore, P., 17, 21
librarians, 28, 60, 83
literature course redesign. *See* world literature course redesign
Luginbuhl, G., 56

Manwaring, M., 16
Mattson, K., 54
McLuhan, Marshal, 17
McMichael, Kelly, 112–121
measurement. *See* assessment
Millennials, 17–19
multidisciplinary approach to course redesign, 55–56, 57
multiple choice items. *See* selected response items

National Center for Academic Transformation, 22
National Survey of Student Engagement, 15
Net Generation, 7, 17–19
neural networks and learning, 9–10, 11, 14
Next Generation course case studies
art history course, 89–101
biology course, 70–78
communicating in business course, 79–88
U.S. history course, 112–121
world literature course, 101–112
Next Generation Course Redesign Project
Blended Learning Projects and, 22–24
Community of Practice and, 26, 28
course goals of, 35–36
Faculty Fellows, 27–35, 59–60
funding of, 27
instructional approaches in, 39–40
meetings of, 30–33
national context of, 21–22
presentations on, 33–34

project goals of, 25–26
Quality Enhancement Plan and, 24–25, 87
request for proposal, 27, 57, 59
retreats of, 29–30
student learning outcomes in, 36
training of faculty in, 29, 34–35, 60
See also course redesign

objectives. *See* goals
online learning activities
in art history course, 96–97
best uses of, 40
in biology course, 70–71, 73–74
in communicating in business course, 80, 84
in U.S. history course, 113–114, 118–119
in world literature course, 101, 102, 105, 108
organic chemistry course redesign activity, 56
Osterlind, S. J., 45
outcome based assessment, 41–51
outcomes. *See* goals

Parini, J., 4
Parker, A., 28
Pasquesi, K., 17, 21
PBL. *See* problem based learning
Pearcy, A. G. *Finding the perfect blend.*, 48
pedagogy
in art history course, 96–98
in biology course, 72–75
in communicating in business course, 81–84
in U.S. history course, 115–119
in world literature course, 104–107
See also lecture-based instruction; online learning activities; small group work
peer recognition for innovation, 86
physics, experiential learning in, 22
Piaget, Jean, 16
plan, assessment, 33, 37–38, 62, 63
plan, test specifications, 44–45
planning, long term, 55–57
planning, short term, 57–58
Preference for Course Format Survey, 48, 77, 84–85, 109–110

Principles of Biology course redesign.
    See biology course redesign
problem based learning, 40, 90–91, 94,
    98, 101
problems in courses, identification of, 54
programs, assessment of, 47–51
project leader, 55
publicity, 33, 58, 63–64

Quality Enhancement Plan, 24, 87

Reason, R., 14
recitation activities, 70, 71, 72, 73, 74–75
redesign, course. *See* course redesign
request for proposal, 27, 57, 59
resistance to change, 4, 53, 112
responses, learner, 13
rewards and recognition for faculty,
    53, 61, 65–66, 112
Riedling, A. M., 10
Rimer, S., 22
role-playing simulations, 113, 115–117,
    120–121
rubrics
    in art history course, 94, 95, 98, 100
    constructed response items and, 37, 47
    in U.S. history course, 115, 121
    in world literature course, 103

scheduling, classroom, 53, 55, 58, 63,
    64–65, 99
score distribution, 46–47, 49
selected response items
    specific learning outcomes and, 49
    student learning outcomes and, 42
    test specification plan and, 44
    training in, 35
    validation of, 45–46
    writing guidelines for, 45
Senior Faculty Fellows
    case studies of redesigned courses and, 69
    Community of Practice and, 111
    definition of, 28
    presentations by, 29, 30, 33, 59, 60
Seymour, E., 5
simulations, role-playing, 113, 115–117,
    120–121

small group work
    in art history course, 90, 97–98
    in biology course, 70, 74–75
    in communicating in business course,
        80, 82, 83–84, 87
    in U.S. history course, 115–117, 120–121
    in world literature course, 101–102,
        105–107, 108, 109
    See also collaborative learning; team
        projects
Smith, T. W., 14
social aspects of learning, 11, 15, 65
space and scheduling, classroom, 53, 55, 58,
    63, 64–65, 99
specific learning outcomes, 43–44, 49
    See also goals
student academic success rates. *See* success
    rates, student
Student as Scholar model, 17
Student Assessment of Learning Gains, 76–77
student attitude toward subject of course,
    survey of, 48, 62, 77, 85, 107–108
student engagement
    about, 14–15
    assessment of, 62
    in communicating in business course, 79,
        80, 82, 84, 85, 86, 87, 88
    goals of course redesign and, 35
    higher level learning and, 7
    national context of course
        redesign and, 21
    National Survey of Student
        Engagement, 15
    teaching strategies and, 39
    in U.S. history course, 117
    in world literature course, 101, 105
student learning outcomes
    about, 35–38, 41–42
    in American government course, 31
    in art history course, 91–95
    in biology course, 71–72, 78
    in communicating in business course,
        80–81, 86
    course redesign administration and, 67
    critical thinking and, 36
    deep learning and, 13–14
    evaluating teaching and, 65
    justifying course redesign and, 62

measurability and, 42
publicity about, 63
Quality Enhancement Plan and, 24
training in, 34, 60
in U.S. history course, 114–115
in world literature course, 102–104, 105
See also goals
student preference for redesign, assessment of, 48, 62, 109–110
student recruiting materials, 64
subject of course, survey of student attitude toward, 48, 62, 77, 85, 107–109
success rates, student
  in art history course, 98–99
  in biology course, 76
  in communicating in business course, 85
  in general education courses, 5, 54
  student engagement and, 14
  in U.S. history course, 119–120
  in world literature course, 110
support, institutional, 58–59, 60–62, 88
support staff, 28, 35
surface learning, 12–13
survey courses, introductory. *See* general education courses
surveys
  Adoption of Courseware Survey for Faculty Members, 50
  Community of Practice Survey, 51
  of course evaluation by department chairs and deans, 50
  of course evaluation by instructor, 50
  Learning Environment Preferences survey, 48–49
  National Survey of Student Engagement, 15
  Preference for Course Format Survey, 48, 77, 84–85, 109–110
  for program purposes evaluation, 50–51
  Survey of Student Attitude Toward Subject of the Course, 48, 62, 77, 85, 107–109
  See also assessment
sustainability and replication of course redesign
  in art history course, 99–100
  in biology course, 77
  in communicating in business course, 86–87
  in U.S. history course, 120–121
  in world literature course, 111

Tang, C. S., 13
Tapscott, D., 4, 17, 18, 19
teachers. *See* faculty
teaching, 13, 14, 39–40
  See also lecture-based instruction; online learning activities; pedagogy; small group work
teaching, rewards and recognition for, 53, 61, 65–66, 112
teaching assistants
  in art history course, 99–100
  in biology course, 77
  in U.S. history course, 120, 121
  in world literature course, 111
team projects, 80, 81, 82, 83–84, 87
  See also small group work
technology
  culture of inquiry and, 17
  lecture-based instruction and, 4
  Net Generation and, 7, 17–19
  support infrastructure for, 58–59
  in world literature course, 102, 111
Terenzini, P., 14
test items, 37–38, 44, 45–47, 49–50
  See also constructed response items; selected response items
tests. *See* assessment
test specification plan, 44–45
thinking, critical. *See* critical thinking
thinking, higher level, 11, 15, 90, 91, 98, 117
training of faculty, 29, 34–35, 60
Transformative Instructional Initiative Project, 57
Turner, P. M., 10

University of North Texas
  Blended Learning Projects, 22–24
  core curriculum, 89, 92, 101
  intellectual property policy, 59
  Next Generation Course Redesign Project (*See* Next Generation Course Redesign Project)

Quality Enhancement Plan, 24–25, 87
Transformative Instructional Initiative
    Project, 57
U.S. history course redesign
    active learning in, 113, 115–117
    assessment in, 113, 114–115, 117, 118
    assessment results of, 119–120
    background of, 112–113
    higher-order thinking in, 117
    lecture-based instruction in, 114, 115
    objectives of, 113
    online learning activities in, 113–114,
        118–119
    role-playing simulations in, 115–117,
        120–121
    small group work in, 115–117, 120–121
    student engagement in, 117
    sustainability and replication of, 120–121
    synopsis of, 113–114
    teaching assistants in, 120, 121

validation of test items, 45–47
Velasquez, B., 28
Vision of Students Today (Wesch), 7

Wesch, Michael, 7
Wieman, Carl, 21–22
Wolfe, P., 9

workload policy, 66
world literature course redesign
    assessment in, 102–104, 105
    assessment results of, 107–111
    background of, 101
    and Community of Practice, 111–112
    costs of, 110–111
    course redesign process and, 111–112
    critical thinking in, 101, 108, 109, 112
    experiential learning in, 101, 105–107,
        110, 112
    higher level learning in, 101, 105,
        106, 107
    lecture-based instruction in, 101, 102,
        104–105
    multidisciplinary approach in, 56
    objectives of, 102–104
    online learning activities in, 101, 102,
        105, 108
    small group work in, 101, 102,
        105–107, 108, 109
    student engagement in, 101, 105
    sustainability and replication of, 111
    synopsis of, 101–102
    teaching assistants in, 111

Zull, J. E., 10, 11, 12